Speaking in Tongues

Speaking in Tongues

by
John MacArthur, Jr.

MOODY PRESS
CHICAGO

All Scripture quotations, unless noted otherwise, are from the *New Scofield Reference Bible*, King James Version. Copyright © 1967 by Oxford University Press, Inc. Reprinted by permission.

Library of Congress Cataloging in Publication Data

MacArthur, John, 1939-
    Speaking in tongues / by John MacArthur, Jr.
       p.   cm. — (John MacArthur's Bible studies)
    Includes indexes.
    ISBN 0-8024-5363-5
    1. Bible. N.T. Corinthians, 1st, XIII, 8-XIV, 40—Criticism, interpretation, etc. 2. Love—Biblical teaching. 3. Glossolalia-Biblical teaching. I. Title. II. Series: MacArthur, John, 1939-Bible studies.
BS2675.2.M294   1988
234'.13—dc19   88—10338
                                                  CIP

1 2 3 4 5 6 7 Printing/LC/Year 93 92 91 90 89 88

Printed in the United States of America

Contents

These Bible studies are taken from messages delivered by Pastor-Teacher John MacArthur, Jr., at Grace Community Church in Panorama City, California. The recorded messages themselves may be purchased as a series or individually. Please request the current price list by writing to:

WORD OF GRACE COMMUNICATIONS
P.O. Box 4000
Panorama City, CA 91412

Or call the following toll-free number:
1-800-55-GRACE

1
The Permanence of Love—Part 1

Outline

Introduction
A. The Corruption in Corinth
  1. In the city
  2. In the church
B. The Correction by Paul
C. The Crescendo of Love
  1. The particulars defined
    a) "Love"
    b) "Faileth"
    c) "Never"
  2. The problem delineated
    a) Love rejected
    b) Love realized

Lesson
  I. The Prominence of Love (vv. 1-3)
 II. The Perfections of Love (vv. 4-7)
III. The Permanence of Love (vv. 8-12)
   A. Gifts Are Temporary—Love Is Eternal (v. 8)
    1. The context of the gifts
    2. The clarification of the gifts
      a) The gift of prophecy
      b) The gift of knowledge
      c) The gift of tongues
    3. The cessation of the gifts
      a) The inherent disagreement
      b) The important distinctions

        (1) The different words used
          (a) *Katargeō*
          (b) *Pauō*
        (2) The different voices used
          (a) Passive voice
          (b) Middle voice
     c) The inevitable deduction

An In-Depth Look at the Modern Tongues Movement
I. An Evaluation of the Cessation of Tongues
  A. The Reasons Tongues Ceased in the Apostolic Age
    1. The gift of tongues was a miraculous gift, and the age of miracles ended with the apostles
      a) The periods of miracles
      b) The passing away of miracles
      c) The purpose of miracles
    2. The miraculous gift of tongues was a judicial sign to Israel because of her unbelief
    3. The gift of tongues was inferior to the gift of prophecy
    4. Speaking in tongues was rendered useless when the New Testament was complete
    5. Tongues are mentioned only in the earliest New Testament books
    6. History records that the gift of tongues ceased in the apostolic age
      a) The significant obscurity of tongues in the writings of the early church Fathers
      b) The supposed occurrences of tongues since the apostolic age
        (1) Outside mainline Christianity
          (a) Montanus and Tertullian
          (b) The Cevenols
          (c) The Jansenists
          (d) The Shakers
          (e) The Irvingites
        (2) Within mainline Christianity
          (a) Pentecostalism
          (b) The charismatic movement

Introduction

First Corinthians 13:8 introduces the subject of tongues and raises the question of whether this gift has ceased. As we proceed into chapter 14, we will become more involved in this subject because it is the theme of that chapter. This is a vital area of information and study that we need to comprehend. But to do that we must spend time carefully examining the biblical evidence. It is difficult to evaluate the validity of speaking in tongues any other way than to go carefully through the Word of God to see how it speaks to the issue.

In 1 Corinthians 13:8-13 Paul says, "Love never faileth; but whether there be prophecies, they shall be done away; whether there be tongues, they shall cease; whether there be knowledge, it shall vanish away. For we know in part, and we prophesy in part. But when that which is perfect is come, then that which is in part shall be done away. When I was a child, I spoke as a child, I understood as a child, I thought as a child; but when I became a man, I put away childish things. For now we see in a mirror, darkly; but then, face to face; now I know in part, but then shall I know even as also I am known. And now abideth faith, hope, love, these three, but the greatest of these is love."

Love. What a wonderful word! First Corinthians 13 has been a favorite passage of many Christians for years—but it also speaks pointedly to the church as a whole. Although we will develop this passage in relation to the tongues issue, Paul's major point is that only love is permanent. The Corinthians needed to hear that because they were so busy fracturing the fellowship over the temporary issues and forgetting what was eternal.

A. The Corruption in Corinth

1. In the city

The Corinthian church existed in a city that was known as the vanity fair of the world. The believers in Corinth were called by God to represent the Lord Jesus Christ and to be a demonstration of His incomparable character. It was a high calling—a calling that could be fulfilled only if they were submissive to His will. The city of Corinth was dominated by materialism, antagonism, competition, selfishness, hatred, and sexual immorality. In that environment the Corinthian believers were to act as salt and light. But unfortunately they did not.

2. In the church

The tragedy of the Corinthian church was that the city of Corinth had salted the church instead of the church salting the city. The corrupt spirit of Corinth had permeated the church. It was evangelism in reverse. The Christians had become carnal, worldly, indulgent, selfish, contentious, vengeful, proud, and compromising. Almost everything that was characteristic of the society had been picked up by the church. In fact, they even perverted their own spiritual behavior into pagan-like religion—twisting spiritual gifts away from the Spirit and operating them in the flesh, under the energy of Satan and his hosts.

B. The Correction by Paul

First Corinthians was written by Paul as a corrective. It is strong, firm, and straightforward. In chapter 13 the apostle Paul climaxes his thoughts about their particular need by essentially saying, "Here is the brightest spot of all—love." That was what was needed in their church. There wasn't any self-sacrificial giving or washing of each other's feet. Rather, the Christians resented each other, argued with each other, and shut each other out from their private groups. They sexually violated each other, sued each other, boasted against each other, deprived each other in marriage, divorced each other, perverted the proper place of women within the church meeting, withheld food from the poor at the love feast, turned the Lord's Table into a drunken orgy, offended each other, and fought each other for prominence in the use of their spiritual gifts.

All those things were evidence of the absence of the one thing needed: love. Paul writes of love in verses 8-12, in effect saying, "You'd better concentrate on love, because that's what really matters; that's what is eternal. Rather than being so concerned that you receive the prominent, showy gifts and the chief place of recognition, be concerned about love. Rather than becoming bitter, antagonistic, and jealous because your gift isn't what someone else has, seek to love, because love never fails."

C. The Crescendo of Love

1. The particulars defined

Let's look at the beginning of verse 8, "Love never faileth."

a) "Love"

The word *love* is defined in verses 4-7.

b) "Faileth"

The common translation of the Greek word translated "faileth" is "to fall." Literally it means "to fall to the ground," and sometimes it refers to the finality of something falling into decay. For example, it is used to speak of the petals of a flower that drop to the ground. This particular word could also be translated "abolished." Love will never be abolished or fall to the ground in decay. Love is a flower in which there is no decay. And because love is synonymous with God (1 John 4:8b), it can never cease, because in Him there is no such thing as decay.

c) "Never"

The Greek word translated "never" has to do with time. What it really says is: "Love, at no time, will ever fail." I believe that someday love will be the only

11

thing left. When we get to heaven, we won't need teaching anymore because we'll know everything. We won't need preaching anymore because we'll have already responded in obedience. We won't need anyone to hold us up, or help us, or rebuke us, or exhort us, or encourage us, or pray for us, or do anything else for us. Why? Because we'll be like Jesus Christ. The one thing that will remain, however, is love—in a dimension we've never dreamed of. We'll be totally involved in the character of God's love as it's manifested through each of us to one another forever.

Paul was saying to the Corinthians, "You ought to get a grip on what will be around forever and quit quibbling over what is temporary."

2. The problem delineated

The phrase "love never faileth" is often misunderstood and misapplied. For example, some people believe that it means "love always succeeds and wins in every situation." They believe that with love everything will turn out all right. I don't believe that is what Paul was saying for the following reasons.

a) Love rejected

Paul went into many towns and loved many people —but he still was thrown out of almost every town he entered. The Lord Jesus Christ loved with an incomparable love—yet the world refused it, rejected it, spurned it, and walked out of His presence. The rich young ruler was granted an occasion to sense and receive the love of Jesus Christ—but he turned away from it. That must have been a great disappointment to Jesus, but I imagine His greatest disappointment was Judas. Judas basked in the sunlight of Christ's love for three years and then turned his back on it. This is true in marriage as well. Many husbands have turned their backs on the love of their wives, and many wives have turned their backs on the love of their husbands. Love doesn't always win out in that sense. But that is not what Paul was saying.

b) Love realized

> Paul was saying that love is eternal. And because it will go on forever, that is where we need to put our emphasis. That's a great message for the church. If we could simplify the whole idea of the church, it would be for everyone to love everyone else. If everyone loves everyone else, then believers will minister to one another in love, and Christ will be visible in the world. Once that happens no one would be able to stop the flood of unbelieving people coming to discover what is happening. Paul was simply saying, "Love is the bottom line in the life of the church."

As I discuss the tongues movement, I'm dealing with it from a theological and biblical perspective, not a personal one. Please understand that even though I might not agree with all of the things that are going on in that movement, the emphasis of 1 Corinthians 13 rings loud in my heart. My attitude (and yours) toward anyone in the fellowship of Christ is to be one of love. I simply want to clarify some issues that sometimes haven't been looked at carefully in the light of Scripture.

Lesson

In 1 Corinthians 13:1-7 Paul discusses four different features of love. The first two features of love are:

 I. THE PROMINENCE OF LOVE (vv. 1-3)

 II. THE PERFECTIONS OF LOVE (vv. 4-7)

Now we'll look at Paul's third point.

III. THE PERMANENCE OF LOVE (vv. 8-12)

The phrase that begins verse 8, "Love never faileth," basically sums up the whole issue for the rest of the chapter. Everything else that is said comments, modifies, and does an exposition on that statement. Love never fails. Hope will come to an end because it will one day be realized. Faith will also come to an end because it will be actualized. We'll have sight instead. Love, however, will never come to an end. It will go on forever. The Bible doesn't say that God is hope or that God is faith. But the Bible does say that God is love (1 John 4:8b). Love is as eternal as God.

To make his point about the permanence of love, Paul contrasted love with three gifts and showed: (1) that gifts are temporary but love is eternal, (2) that gifts are partial but love is complete, and (3) that gifts are elementary but love is mature.

A. Gifts Are Temporary—Love Is Eternal (v. 8)

"Love never faileth; but whether there be prophecies, they shall be done away; whether there be tongues, they shall cease; whether there be knowledge, it shall vanish away."

Paul said that three important gifts will cease: prophecy, tongues, and knowledge. They existed for a limited time, in contrast to the eternal nature of love. And although love is indispensable in the use of the gifts, it's going to outlast them.

1. The context of the gifts

Paul used spiritual gifts to contrast love, because gifts were highly prized in the Corinthian church. The Corinthians were proud, self-seeking, and self-centered. They were spiritual show-offs—desiring to be in an upfront position. To them the gifts were important. They showed off their spirituality by demonstrating their gifts. As it turned out, the gifts they demonstrated were for the most part fleshly or satanic counterfeits. Nevertheless, that is where they put their emphasis.

It's interesting to realize that in the entire letter of 1 Corinthians (sixteen chapters), there is not a single mention of an elder or a leader of that church. Apparently no one was leading. In fact, they had come to the place where their whole view of church worship was the philosophy "We'll just come together and let the Holy Spirit do His thing and let it all happen." Finally in 14:32 the apostle Paul cries out, "The spirits of the prophets are subject to the prophets." Then in 14:40 he says, "Let all things be done decently and in order." A church can't operate without leaders. God never intended for the church to be a group of people who gather together and do whatever they feel like doing. The church is to have structure and order, because God is a God of order.

The Corinthian church had no leadership or order. Instead, they had decided to fight over who would be the most prominent. Paul in effect said, "These gifts that you have exalted, these independent expressions of so-called spirituality, are all temporary—even the true ones. However, love will go on forever. Love is the more excellent way."

2. The clarification of the gifts

   a) The gift of prophecy

      "Whether there be prophecies, they shall be done away."

      The plural word *prophecies* makes reference to the result of the gift of prophecy—many prophecies. Basically this gift was the ability to proclaim God's truth publicly. The Greek word for prophecy comes from the two Greek words *pro* (meaning "before") and *phēmi* (meaning "to speak"). It literally means "to speak before." Its primary use is "to speak before an audience" (forthtelling), not "to speak before" in terms of time (foretelling). The gift of prophecy, then, was to speak before people, proclaiming the Word of God. The purpose of this gift is indicated in 1 Corinthians 14:3, where Paul says, "He that prophesieth speaketh unto men to edification, and exhortation, and comfort." Someone with this gift speaks to build others up, to encourage them to good behavior, and to comfort them in their trouble. That is the gift of prophecy.

b) The gift of knowledge

"Whether there be knowledge, it shall vanish away."

The second gift that Paul mentions is the gift of knowledge. It's called "the word of knowledge" in 1 Corinthians 12:8 because it is considered to be a speaking gift—one that the Corinthians would have celebrated as a public gift. The gift of knowledge is defined as "the ability to observe facts and to draw spiritual truth out of the Word of God." It is the gift of being able to understand God's Word. Seen as a scholar's or teacher's gift, the Corinthians considered it a prominent gift.

c) The gift of tongues

The third gift mentioned by Paul in 1 Corinthians 13:8 is the gift of tongues, or languages. Throughout these studies I will use those terms synonymously so that you will understand that even though tongues is the word that is being used today, the literal meaning of the Greek term *glōssa* is "languages." We will see in our study of 1 Corinthians 14 that tongues always refers to a known language. Briefly, then, the definition of the gift of tongues is "the ability to speak a foreign language that had not been learned by the speaker." Its purpose, as we will see, was as a sign of God's judgment to unbelieving Jews.

3. The cessation of the gifts

Verse 8 clearly states that these three prominent gifts —prophecy, knowledge, and tongues—are going to come to an end. The question is when.

a) The inherent disagreement

My Pentecostal and charismatic brothers and sisters in Christ say that none of these three gifts have ceased. Their answer to the question of when is, "In the future." Some of them say that these gifts will cease when the perfection mentioned in verse 10 comes—which they see as future as well. At the other end of the spectrum, I've heard others say that all the gifts have already ceased. They don't believe there are any spiritual gifts today. Those are the two extreme viewpoints: all the gifts are in effect today, or none of them are in effect today. There is also a third view that says some of the gifts are now in effect and some of them are not. Which view is correct? Let's look at the Bible to see.

A Weak Argument to Prove That All the Gifts Are Still in Effect

Those who say that all the gifts are still in effect today often give the following argument. They say, "There isn't one verse in the entire Bible that says tongues have ceased." That's true—there isn't a single verse in the Bible that specifically states that tongues have ceased. But there isn't a single verse in the Bible that specifically states that God is three in one, either. But He is. To argue that something isn't true because the Bible doesn't specifically say it is true is a weak argument. And to argue that one needs a specific biblical statement to prove a point is also weak. Why? Because there are many truths in the Bible that are indicated to us by the totality of Scripture rather than by any one given statement. For example, there isn't a verse that specifically says, "Jesus is 100 percent God and 100 percent man at the same time in an indivisible oneness." But that is the essence of the God-Man character of Christ. We have to piece together all the biblical facts of Christ's character to see the whole portrait. Therefore to argue that tongues haven't ceased because there isn't a verse specifically stating that fact is not a good argument to use.

b) The important distinctions

According to verse 8, all the gifts are going to cease sometime. They're all going to be rendered inoperative. But if you look at verse 8 more carefully, you'll discover some important distinctions that the apostle Paul and the Holy Spirit make between tongues, prophecy, and knowledge. The different Greek words that are used indicate that tongues will cease at a different point in time than prophecy and knowledge. This is an important distinction.

17

(1) The different words used

(a) *Katargeō*

The beginning of verse 8 says that prophecies "shall be done away." Other translations say "shall be rendered inoperative" or "abolished." The end of verse 8 says that knowledge "shall vanish away." Those two phrases describing the cessation of prophecy and knowledge are translating the same Greek verb, *katargeō*, which means "to be made inoperative." However, that is not the verb used in reference to the cessation of tongues. A totally different word is used.

(b) *Pauō*

There is a purpose in the mind of the Holy Spirit for making a distinction with these two terms, and I want you to understand what it is. Knowledge and prophecy will be rendered inoperative, but tongues "will cease." This is indicated by the use of a different Greek verb —*pauō*—which means "to stop."

The first distinction that is made in verse 8 is the use of two different Greek words to describe the cessation of prophecy and knowledge and the cessation of tongues.

(2) The different voices used

(a) Passive voice

The verb *katargeō*, in describing the cessation of prophecy and knowledge, is in the passive voice. The rule of grammar states that when a passive verb is in a sentence, the subject receives the action. In the case of prophecy and knowledge, something will act upon them to cause them to stop. What is it that's going to do that? Look at verses 9-10: "For we know in part [the gift of knowledge], and we prophesy in part [the gift of prophecy]. But when that which is perfect is come, then that which is in part shall be done away [Gk., *katargeō*]." What is it that's going to come and stop prophecy and knowledge? "That which is perfect." Also notice that tongues do not appear in verse 9. Why? Because only prophecy and knowledge are stopped by "that which is perfect."

(b) Middle voice

The verb that says tongues will cease (*pauō*) is in the middle voice. There are differences among the active, passive, and middle voices. In the active voice we would say, "I hit the ball." In the passive voice we would say, "The ball hit me." And in the middle voice (if English had a middle voice) we would say, "I hit myself." In other words, the Greek middle voice is reflexive, indicating that the subject is acting upon itself. The middle voice also indicates intense action on the part of the subject. Literally, then, verse 8 says, "Tongues will stop by themselves." That's the meaning that the middle voice gives to the verb *pauō*.

The Septuagint (the Greek translation of the Old Testament) uses the middle form of *pauō* fifteen times to translate the Hebrew word that means "to complete," "to stop," "to finish," "to accomplish," "to end." It has a finality to it. And the reflexive middle voice gives it the idea that it ends all by itself.

c) The inevitable deduction

The gifts of prophecy and knowledge, then, are going to continue on until "that which is perfect" comes and stops them. The gift of tongues is going to stop all by itself. That's what has to be deduced when one looks at the Greek text.

I. AN EVALUATION OF THE CESSATION OF TONGUES

If tongues are going to stop by themselves, the next question is when. After spending many years studying this question and reading all sides of the issue, and after spending many hours discussing it with charismatics and trying to evaluate it from their perspective, I am convinced beyond all reasonable doubt that tongues ceased in the apostolic age nineteen hundred years ago. And I also believe that the word *pauō* indicates that once tongues stopped, they stopped forever.

A. The Reasons Tongues Ceased in the Apostolic Age

1. The gift of tongues was a miraculous gift, and the age of miracles ended with the apostles

a) The periods of miracles

I'm not saying that God doesn't do wonderful things. I'm not saying that God doesn't heal. And I'm not saying that God doesn't act providentially to put together things that would be humanly impossible. However, throughout God's redemptive history, there have only been three distinct periods of time that miracles were prominent. And in each of these periods, the miracles were for the specific purpose of confirming God's Word. These three periods were the period of Moses and Joshua (1441-1370 B.C.), the period of Elijah and Elisha (870-785 B.C.), and the period of Christ and the apostles (A.D. 28-90). Between these periods of miracles, each of which lasted approximately seventy years, there were long periods of time where miracles either did not happen at all or happened infrequently. The few miracles that did occur between the specific periods of miracles could in no way be considered the norm.

I believe that the miracles that occurred in the time of Christ and the apostles were simply foretastes of "the powers of the age to come" (Heb. 6:5). The "age to come" refers to the millennial kingdom, not the church age. At certain intervals in God's redemptive history He cut a hole in the coming kingdom and let some of its character leak out—tastes of what was to come. It was never God's intention, however, to let miracles run riot throughout all redemptive history.

b) The passing away of miracles

The last recorded miracle in the New Testament occurred around A.D. 58 with the healing of Publius's father (Acts 28:7-10). From that date to A.D. 96, when John finished Revelation, there is no record of any miracles occurring. The miraculous gifts, like tongues and healing, are mentioned only in the earlier book of 1 Corinthians. When the gifts are discussed in later books such as Ephesians and Romans, there is no mention of these gifts. God, in His wonderful design, had a purpose for miracles.

c) The purpose of miracles

The apostles were part of a miraculous age that confirmed His Word. They were involved in offering the kingdom to Israel and giving them a taste of the miracles and powers of the age to come—letting them sample the kingdom. That is what the writer of Hebrews was talking about when he basically said to his Jewish readers, "When you have turned your back on the kingdom you have sampled, there isn't any hope for you. It's impossible for you to be renewed again to repentance once you have tasted the powers of the age to come and turned your back on them" (Heb. 6:4-6). Once Israel turned its back on God, He turned from Israel to the Gentiles. At that point, the purpose of those miracles as a sign to Israel had ended. That's an important truth to understand!

A text that is vital to our thinking is Hebrews 2:3-4. The writer of Hebrews was writing to Jewish people who had come to a knowledge of Christ and were deeply considering whether they would submit to Him as their Savior and Lord. In other words, they were riding the fence. The writer of Hebrews said to them, "How shall we escape, if we neglect so great salvation, which at the first began to be spoken by the Lord, and was confirmed unto us by them that heard him [the apostles], God also bearing them witness, both with signs and wonders, and with diverse miracles and gifts of the Holy Spirit."

Notice that the writer of Hebrews uses the past tense in verse 3 when he says that the gospel "was confirmed." By the time Hebrews was written (before the destruction of Jerusalem in A.D. 70), the gospel, or doctrine of salvation, had already been confirmed by signs, wonders, diverse miracles, and gifts of the Spirit—supernatural manifestations proving its divine origin. It's interesting to me that even by that time, the writer of Hebrews viewed these confirming miracles as something in the past.

I believe that God is a God of miracles. I believe He can do whatever He wants, whenever He wants. However, the constant dialogue I'm hearing about the massive outbreak of miracles in our day doesn't fit the biblical pattern.

2. The miraculous gift of tongues was a judicial sign to Israel because of her unbelief

In 1 Corinthians 14:21 Paul quotes Isaiah 28:11-12, saying, "In the law it is written, With men of other tongues and other lips will I speak unto this people; and yet for all that will they not hear me, saith the Lord." In this prophecy to Israel, God was saying, "Israel, I have spoken to you in clear words, but you haven't listened to Me. Therefore, as a sign confirming your unbelief, I will begin to speak to you in a language you won't be able to understand." The gift of tongues was part of God's judicial act of telling Israel that He was turning aside from her to the church. He had offered the Israelites the kingdom, but they had refused it. They had refused and executed their King, their long-awaited Messiah. As a judicial sign of Israel's violation, God spoke to His people with other tongues and other lips.

22

The gift of tongues had a primary significance to Israel. In fact, in 1 Corinthians 14:22 Paul says, "Wherefore, tongues are for a sign, not to them that believe, but to them that believe not." The gift of tongues was never intended for Christians; it was intended as a judicial sign to Israel. Once God's judgment had fallen on Israel, the gift of tongues would have no significance at all. God's judicial act against them came in A.D. 70 when Titus Vespasian, the Roman conqueror, swept down and destroyed Jerusalem. And the gift of tongues, which was a sign to unbelieving Israel of God's judicial act against them, also came to an end because it was no longer needed.

3. The gift of tongues was inferior to the gift of prophecy

When tongues were interpreted, they had the ability to edify (1 Cor. 14:5). Uninterpreted, tongues were a sign against Israel; but to give it some meaning in the church, they had to be interpreted. However, this potential for edification was not its main purpose. Once Israel had been judged, the purpose of tongues as a judicial sign ceased. I've heard people say, "Even though the gift of tongues is no longer a judicial sign, it still has the potential to edify the church." That is unnecessary, because the gift of prophecy is far superior to the gift of tongues as an expression of edification. First Corinthians 14:1 says, "Follow after love, and desire spiritual gifts, but rather that ye may prophesy." In fact, in chapter 14, Paul proves that the gift of tongues is an inferior means of communication (vv. 1-12), an inferior method of praise (vv. 13-19), and an inferior method of evangelism (vv. 20-25). In verse 19 of the same chapter Paul says, "I had rather speak five words with my understanding . . . than ten thousand words in an unknown tongue." There is no reason to exalt the gift of tongues. It has no continuing edifying purpose that can't be better accompanied by prophecy (preaching). That's the point of chapter 14.

4. Speaking in tongues was rendered useless when the New Testament was complete

Another characteristic of the gift of tongues was that when a person spoke in tongues and had it interpreted, that was a direct revelation from God. Has direct revelation from God ceased? Yes (Jude 3). Is there any more to Scripture than what we now have? No. In fact, at the end of the last book of the Bible, the apostle John wrote, "I testify unto every man that heareth the words of the prophecy of this book, If any man shall add unto these things, God shall add unto him the plagues that are written in this book" (Rev. 22:18). Tongues as a revelatory source ceased to have the meaning that they had in the infancy of the church—when God was giving revelations before the Bible was complete.

Hebrews 1:1-2 says, "God, who at sundry times and in diverse manners spoke in time past unto the fathers by the prophets, hath in these last days spoken unto us by his Son." In these last days we have been given the Word of the Son—the New Testament. There is no further revelation.

5. Tongues are mentioned only in the earliest New Testament books

It's interesting that 1 Corinthians is the only epistle where the gift of tongues appears. Paul wrote at least twelve other epistles and never even mentioned it, and James, John, and Jude never mentioned it. The gift of tongues disappeared. Even though it has always been the mystical dream throughout history that God would give a private revelation of Himself to each individual, it hasn't happened. God gave His Word and then authenticated it. What we now have is "the faith which was once [for all] delivered unto the saints" (Jude 3b). Revelation has ended. Tongues as a revelatory, edifying, sign gift has ceased to have any function.

First Corinthians 13:8 says that tongues will cease. That's not even a point to argue about. And we've already seen that the word *pauō* in verse 8 has a sense of finality to it—meaning that once tongues stopped, they would never begin again. An important question to answer, then, is, Since the apostolic age, has the gift of tongues ever ceased?

6. History records that the gift of tongues ceased in the apostolic age

The first revival of tongues within the confines of the evangelical church of Jesus Christ since the apostolic age was in 1901. Where had it been for eighteen hundred years? Does 1 Corinthians 13:8 say that tongues will cease and then start up again? No. Tongues ceased— never to begin again. Their purpose was accomplished.

a) The significant obscurity of tongues in the writings of the early church Fathers

The post-apostolic Fathers were the church leaders who lived immediately after the apostolic age. If you study their writings, you'll discover something significant—they don't discuss the gift of tongues. Cleon Rogers, a scholar and missionary, wrote, "It is significant that the gift of tongues is nowhere alluded to, hinted at, or even found in any writings of the Post-Apostolic Fathers" ("The Gift of Tongues in the Post-Apostolic Church," *Bibliotheca Sacra*, 122:134).

(1) Clement of Rome (A.D. 88-97) wrote a letter to the Corinthians in A.D. 95 discussing their spiritual problems. He didn't mention tongues, because apparently the gift had ceased. The gift of tongues, then, wasn't an issue by A.D. 95.

(2) Justin Martyr (A.D. 100-165) was a great church Father who traveled throughout the churches and wrote many things defending Christianity, but he never mentioned tongues. He made lists of spiritual gifts that did not include the gift of tongues.

(3) Origen (A.D. 185-253) was a widely read scholar without equal in the minds of some. In all the volumes he wrote, there is no mention of tongues.

25

And in his apologetic against Celsus, he explicitly argued that the signs of the apostolic age were temporary and that no contemporary Christian exercised any of the ancient prophetical gifts.

(4) Chrysostom (A.D. 347-407) was perhaps the greatest of all the ancient Christian writers. In his *Homilies on First Corinthians*, he makes the following comment on chapter 12: "This whole place is very obscure; but the obscurity is produced by our ignorance of the facts referred to and by their cessation, being such as then used to occur, but now no longer take place" ("Homilies on First Corinthians," *The Nicene and Post-Nicene Fathers*, vol. 12, ed. Philip Schaff [New York: Christian Literature Co., 1888]). In other words, by the end of the fourth century Chrysostom indicated that because tongues didn't exist anymore, the gift was difficult to define or understand.

(5) Augustine (A.D. 354-430) made the following comment on Acts 2:4: "In the earliest times, 'the Holy Ghost fell upon them that believed: and they spake with tongues,' . . . These were signs adapted to the time. For there behooved to be that betokening of the Holy Spirit. . . . That thing was done for a betokening, and it passed away" ("Ten Homilies on the First Epistle of John," *The Nicene and Post-Nicene Fathers*, vol. 7, ed. Philip Schaff [New York: Christian Literature Co., 1888]).

The greatest theologians of the ancient church considered the gift of tongues a remote practice. By the fourth century they didn't understand what it was anymore.

b) The supposed occurrences of tongues since the apostolic age

(1) Outside mainline Christianity

(*a*) Montanus and Tertullian

During the period of the early church Fathers, the only people in the church who were reported to have spoken in tongues were the followers of Montanus and Tertullian. In the middle of the second century, Montanus, a pagan priest who had been recently converted to Christianity, announced to everyone that he was the spokesman for the Holy Spirit. Believing that Christ was soon going to set up the kingdom with headquarters in his hometown of Phrygia, he tried to justify speaking in tongues as an occurrence of the end of the age. He was accompanied by two female priestesses, Prisca and Maximilla, who also spoke in ecstatic speech. Montanus was thrown out of the church as a heretic. Tertullian, a disciple of Montanus, advocated speaking in tongues as well. He lived from A.D. 150-222.

There are other occasions of tongues, or ecstatic speech, during this period—but not in Christianity. Tongues were characteristic of pagan religions (e.g., the priestesses of Delphi, pagan witch doctors, and various seers), but they were not present in Christianity.

After Montanus and Tertullian, the next eruption of tongues wasn't until the late seventeenth century.

(*b*) The Camisards of Cévennes

The gift of ecstatic utterance was claimed by a group of persecuted Protestants in southern France around 1685. They believed that their little children, who knew only the local dialect, were able to speak in perfect French while in a trance. The group was soon discredited because of their night raids and military reprisals against their enemies. And because all their prophecies went unfulfilled, they were branded as heretics and not considered to be a part of mainline Christianity.

(c) The Jansenists

Around 1731 extremists of the Roman Catholic reformers called the Jansenists were holding night meetings at their leader's tomb, during which time they supposedly spoke in ecstatic languages.

(d) The Shakers

The Shakers were the followers of Mother Ann Lee, who lived from 1736-84. She regarded herself as the female equivalent of Jesus Christ—God in a female body. She founded the first Shaker community in America in New Lebanon, New York. Lee claimed she had received a revelation from God that sexual intercourse was corrupt, even within marriage. It is said that to teach her followers to mortify the flesh and resist temptation, she instituted the practice of men and women's dancing together in the nude while they spoke in tongues!

(e) The Irvingites

Around 1830 Edward Irving started a little group in London known as the Irvingites. This group began to speak in tongues but was soon discredited for several reasons. Their revelations contradicted Scripture, their prophecies went unfulfilled, their supposed healings were followed by death, there were rumors of immorality, and some of the leading members were accused of fraud.

All these groups that supposedly spoke in tongues were not part of genuine Christianity. At the start of the twentieth century, however, speaking in tongues moved into mainline Christianity.

(2) Within mainline Christianity

(*a*) Pentecostalism

The first time tongues became part of mainline Christianity since the apostolic age was in 1901 at Bethel Bible College in Topeka, Kansas. Agnes Ozman received what she called "the baptism of the Holy Spirit" accompanied by estatic utterances. The practice became part of the holiness movement of the church in America. In 1906, estatic utterances came to Azusa Street in Los Angeles, California. Out of these two events in 1901 and 1906 grew the mainline Pentecostal denominations that many of our brothers and sisters in Christ are a part of today. Unlike many of their predecessors, Pentecostals believe the Word of God and preach it. But this particular movement within mainline Christianity didn't begin until the start of this century.

(*b*) The charismatic movement

In 1960 in Van Nuys, California, the modern charismatic movement (characterized by tongues outside of Pentecostal denominations) began in an Episcopalian church. It soon spread across mainline denominations of all kinds.

I have pointed all this out to show you that the true gift of tongues is not something that has gone on throughout history. The Holy Spirit, through the apostle Paul in 1 Corinthians 13:8, said that the biblical gift of tongues would cease. It did, and there's no good reason to believe it has come back.

I have some dear friends who speak in estatic utterances, and they will continue to be my friends. I will always love them. In fact, I have less of a problem with that than I do with gossiping that goes on in a language that is understood. But God has called me to teach His Word, and I am committed to doing so accurately. I know that the theme of 1 Corinthians 13 is love, but love must be exercised within the confines of the truth. And that's what I am attempting to do.

Focusing on the Facts

1. How would you describe the city of Corinth as it existed in Paul's day (see pp. 9-10)?
2. What was the overall tragedy of the Corinthian church? What were some of its specific problems (see p. 10)?
3. All the problems in the Corinthian church can be attributed to the absence of _____ (see p. 10).
4. What does Paul mean by the statement in 1 Corinthians 13:8, "Love never faileth"? How do we know that it doesn't mean that love always wins out in every situation (see pp. 11-13)?
5. In 1 Corinthians 13 what three spiritual gifts does Paul contrast with love to illustrate its permanency? Why did he use spiritual gifts to make his point (see p. 14)?
6. How would you describe the leadership of the Corinthian church (see pp. 14-15)?
7. What is the definition of the gift of prophecy? What is the purpose of that gift (see p. 15)?
8. What is the definition of the gift of knowledge? Why was this gift considered important by the Corinthian church (see p. 16)?
9. What is the definition of the gift of tongues? What was its purpose (see p. 16)?
10. What is the future of the spiritual gifts mentioned in 1 Corinthians 13:8 (see p. 16)?
11. What are the three basic views as to when the gifts of 1 Corinthians 13:8 are going to end (see pp. 16-17)?
12. First Corinthians 13:8 makes two distinctions between how the gifts of prophecy and knowledge will cease and how the gift of tongues will cease. What is the difference in the way these gifts will cease, and how does verse 8 show this distinction (see pp. 17-19)?

13. According to 1 Corinthians 13:10, when are the gifts of prophecy and knowledge going to cease (see pp. 18-19)?
14. When did the gift of tongues cease? What are the six reasons that prove that the gift of tongues ceased at this time (see pp. 20-30)?
15. How many periods in history could be considered as special periods of miracles? What was the purpose of the miracles in each of these periods? Who were the key figures representing each of these periods (see p. 20)?
16. The miracles that occurred during the time of Christ and the apostles were a preview of what future time (see pp. 20-21)?
17. What important truths regarding the miraculous sign gifts are taught in Hebrews 2:3-4 (see pp. 21-22)?
18. What did speaking in tongues signify to unbelieving Jews (see pp. 22-23)?
19. According to 1 Corinthians 14:22 the gift of tongues was primarily intended for what group of people (see p. 23)?
20. What happened in A.D. 70? Why is this important to a discussion of the gift of tongues (see p. 23)?
21. How were tongues able to edify the church? When did this capacity for edification cease? Why did it cease (see p. 23)?
22. What spiritual gift was superior to the gift of tongues in its ability to edify the church? What is Paul's point in 1 Corinthians 14:19 (see p. 23)?
23. Why did God give direct revelation to the early church? When did He stop giving direct revelation? Why (see p. 24)?
24. What's significant about the fact that the gift of tongues is mentioned only in the early epistle of 1 Corinthians (see pp. 24-25)?
25. How do we know that the gift of tongues was not prevalent in the post-apostolic church (see pp. 25-26)?
26. From the first-century church to 1901, did tongues occur within mainline Christianity? What were some of the groups during this period of time that claimed to speak in tongues (see pp. 27-29)?
27. Since the apostolic age, when did speaking in tongues become part of mainline Christianity? What major denomination was started at that time (see p. 29)?
28. When did the charismatic movement start? How does this movement differ from Pentecostalism (see p. 29)?

Pondering the Principles

1. What effect was the church of Corinth supposed to have on the city of Corinth? What effect did they have? Why? Now think of some of the specific ways that you see the modern church affected by our society. Are there any areas in your own life that are being influenced more by the world's perspective than by God's? If so, what are they? To discover the best way to combat the negative influence of the world, see Psalm 119:9, 11; Romans 12:1-2; and Colossians 3:16a. Commit yourself to removing those things in your life that do not support God's view of life as revealed in His Word. Be sure to spend more time reading and studying His Word and being more involved with those in the Body of Christ (Heb. 10:24-25).

2. Even though the main discussion in this lesson was on the gift of tongues, note that the emphasis of 1 Corinthians 13 is on love. When was the last time that you demonstrated love to another Christian who has a doctrinal persuasion different from yours? Think of someone you know who is a Christian but who holds a different view in the area of spiritual gifts. Now think of a specific way that you can love that person by exercising an act of self-sacrificial service on his behalf. Remember, even though doctrinal differences may arise between members of the Body of Christ, we must still show love to one another. However, this does not mean we are to ignore doctrinal error. First Corinthians 13:6 says that love "rejoices in the truth." One aspect of loving one another is to strive for doctrinal purity by pointing out doctrinal error—not by ignoring it!

2

The Permanence of Love—Part 2

Outline

Introduction
A. The Dominance of Love
   1. Discussed
   2. Defined
   3. Displayed
B. The Departure from Love
C. The Demonstration of Love

Review
  I. The Prominence of Love (vv. 1-3)
 II. The Perfections of Love (vv. 4-7)
III. The Permanence of Love (vv. 8-12)
    A. Gifts Are Temporary—Love Is Eternal (v. 8)

An In-Depth Look at the Modern Tongues Movement
  I. An Evaluation of the Cessation of Tongues
    A. The Reasons Tongues Ceased in the Apostolic Age

Lesson
    B. The Responses of Those Who Say Tongues Are for Today
       1. Tongues never ceased
       2. Tongues started up again
 II. An Examination of the Charismatic Misinterpretation of Joel
     2:28-29
    A. The Context
       1. The setting up of the kingdom (v. 20)
       2. The specific elements of the kingdom (vv. 21-27)
       3. The Spirit's work in the kingdom (vv. 28-29)
       4. The signs preceding the kingdom (vv. 30-31)

Introduction

A. The Dominance of Love

1. Discussed

The Bible teaches that love is the very essence of God, observing that "God is love" (1 John 4:8*b*). The Bible also teaches that the highest expression of love is the Lord Jesus Christ, who "having loved his own who were in the world, he loved them unto the end [lit., "unto perfection"]" (John 13:1*b*). Jesus was the perfect example of one who loves. The kind of love that the Bible talks about is a love that "passeth knowledge" (Eph. 3:19). Only by the Holy Spirit can we comprehend its "breadth, and length, and depth, and height" (Eph. 3:18). This same love of God "is shed abroad in our hearts" (Rom. 5:5).

Love, then, is a dominant theme in Scripture. It is the nature of God expressed in Christ, and it is beyond human understanding. Yet it is poured out in the life of every believer. What a tremendous truth!

2. Defined

Love is not a feeling or an emotion. It is a spirit of self-sacrifice. It is a willingness to meet another's need—even if it means sacrificing something we need or possess.

3. Displayed

Love is to be such a dominating characteristic in the life of a Christian—such a way of life—that a Christian should be recognized by virtue of his love. In John 13:35 that's essentially what Jesus says: "By this shall all men know that ye are my disciples, if ye have love one to another." This is reiterated in 1 John. For example, "He that saith he is in the light, and hateth his brother, is in darkness even until now. He that loveth his brother abideth in the light" (2:9-10a). In other words, Christians are people who love their brothers. First John 3:16 says, "By this perceive we the love of God, because he laid down his life for us; and we ought to lay down our lives for the brethren." And in 1 John 3:18 John says, "My little children, let us not love in word, neither in tongue, but in deed and in truth."

Our lives, then, are to be characterized by love. It is vital to every believer.

B. The Departure from Love

First Corinthians 13 is an overwhelming chapter discussing the reality of love. I wish I could teach this chapter about love straight through from beginning to end and do nothing but celebrate the greatness of love. Why don't I? Because I get stuck at the word *tongues* (Gk., *glōssa*) in verse 8. And the reason I get stuck at that point is that this is an issue today. I must speak on it. If I had lived a hundred years ago, I would have been able to preach straight through the thirteenth chapter without a hitch. In my discussion of verse 8, I would have simply said, "The word *tongues* refers to a spiritual gift that was present in the apostolic age but is no longer around." I can't say that today, however. It would be nice if we could talk about love and leave it at that. But I believe we have to depart from the main subject of the chapter to deal with the issue of speaking in tongues.

C. The Demonstration of Love

Because the people of the world don't understand love, it's important that we live out God's love in our relationships with them. But it is also important that they see the love we have for one another. This has many applications, one of which is the attitude that we have when we discuss an issue such as speaking in tongues. We must maintain a spirit of love.

When the world says, "I love you," what they are saying is, "I love myself, and what I want is you." The world's love is a selfish love. I remember hearing a story about a girl who was totally despondent. She called up her pastor and said, "What am I going to do? There's a man who loves me so much that he says he'll shoot himself if I don't marry him." The pastor replied, "Don't do anything. Let him shoot himself! Such a threat is not love; it's pure selfishness." That's right. That man wasn't saying, "I love you"; he was saying, "I love myself; therefore, I want you."

The world doesn't understand love, so we have to demonstrate it to them. And it's not as simple as merely loving the world; we must also show the world that we love each other even when we disagree. Christians must love one another! We must realize that those who are involved in the charismatic movement are our brothers and sisters in Christ. We must also keep the perspective that love is what's eternal—gifts are going to pass away. All of that, however, doesn't mean that we are to avoid the issue of speaking in tongues. We have to do what Paul says in Ephesians 4:15 by "speaking the truth in love."

Review

I. THE PROMINENCE OF LOVE (vv. 1-3)

II. THE PERFECTIONS OF LOVE (vv. 4-7)

III. THE PERMANENCE OF LOVE (vv. 8-12)

A. Gifts Are Temporary—Love Is Eternal (v. 8; see pp. 14-19)

"Love never faileth; but whether there be prophecies, they shall be done away [lit., "be rendered inoperative"]; whether there be tongues, they shall cease [lit., "stop by themselves"]; whether there be knowledge, it shall vanish away [lit., "be rendered inoperative"]."

In verse 8 the verb *katargeō* is used to describe what happens in both prophecy and knowledge. Used in its passive form, it means that knowledge and prophecy will be rendered inoperative. In other words, something is going to act upon those two gifts to cause them to cease. The verb used to describe what is going to happen to the gift of tongues is a totally different verb—*pauō*—which means "to stop." Not only is it a different verb, it's in a different voice —the middle voice. The middle voice in the Greek is reflective, indicating that the subject is acting upon itself. It also indicates intense action on the part of the subject. In other words, tongues will stop by themselves. According to 1 Corinthians 13:9-10, knowledge and prophecy are said to be stopped by "that which is perfect." Notice that tongues are not mentioned in those verses. Why not? Because nothing stops tongues—they stop by themselves before "that which is perfect is come."

In our last lesson I departed from the outline of 1 Corinthians 13 to take a closer look at the gift of tongues. Now we'll continue that discussion.

An In-Depth Look at the Modern Tongues Movement

I. AN EVALUATION OF THE CESSATION OF TONGUES

A. The Reasons Tongues Ceased in the Apostolic Age (see pp. 20-30)

In our last lesson we saw that the legitimate gift of tongues has indeed ceased. I gave you six reasons why this is true; however, these six reasons can be summarized into two major points: (1) the purpose for the gift of tongues came to an end, and (2) history records that the gift of tongues ceased.

Lesson

B. The Responses of Those Who Say Tongues Are for Today

It is interesting to see how our charismatic brothers and sisters in Christ respond to the evidence that the gift of tongues has ceased. They usually respond in one of two ways.

1. Tongues never ceased

Some within the charismatic movement point to people like Montanus, Mother Ann Lee, and some of the others who spoke in tongues since the first century, and claim that these people were their forerunners. In doing that, however, they're putting themselves in a heretical tradition and saying, "Our movement has been a part of the heresy of the church for years." I'm not sure that's what they want to say.

The only other alternative, which is the route most of them go, is to admit that tongues ceased but then began again.

2. Tongues started up again

Most charismatics believe that tongues did cease in the first century but that they are starting up again. They say that because we are now in the last days, God is giving us the last-day outpouring of His Spirit. That's more reasonable than the other view; however, it's the same position the heretic Montanus held during the middle of the second century. When he was asked why the gift of tongues suddenly started up with him after having ceased many years before, he said it was because the kingdom of God would be established at any moment with its headquarters near his hometown. In a similar manner we're asking the charismatics where the gift of tongues has been for the last nineteen hundred years, and their reply is, "It's been restored because we are in the last days." If you ask charismatics what Scripture passage they use to back up this last-day phenomenon of speaking in tongues, they will invariably go to Joel 2:28-29.

II. AN EXAMINATION OF THE CHARISMATIC MISINTERPRETATION OF JOEL 2:28-29

"It shall come to pass afterward, that I will pour out my Spirit upon all flesh; and your sons and your daughters shall prophesy, your old men shall dream dreams, your young men shall see visions; and also, upon the servants and upon the handmaids in those days will I pour out my Spirit."

A. The Context

Charismatics say we are now experiencing the last-day outpouring of the Holy Spirit. However, there are several problems with that. First of all, this passage must be looked at in its prophetic context. According to verse 31, the context is "the great and the terrible day of the Lord." In other words, the general context is the second coming of Christ. Joel 2, then, is dealing with an end-time prophecy. Let's look at more of the specifics of this chapter.

1. The setting up of the kingdom (v. 20)

   In verse 20 the Lord says to Israel, "I will remove far off from you the northern army, and will drive him into a land barren and desolate." In what period of time is Israel confronted by a northern army? During the Great Tribulation (Dan. 11:40), but this northern army will be defeated when Christ comes in the great victory of Armageddon. What happens immediately after Armageddon? Christ judges the nations and sets up His kingdom. The northern army is defeated in verse 20, then verse 21 introduces the kingdom.

2. The specific elements of the kingdom (vv. 21-27)

   The land of Israel will be under a terrible siege that will result in unbelievable bloodshed. In fact, Revelation 14:20 says that the blood from the Battle of Armageddon will be as deep as a horse's bridle for a distance of two hundred miles. Beginning in Joel 2:21, the kingdom is introduced: "Fear not, O land. Be glad and rejoice; for the Lord will do great things. Be not afraid, ye beasts of the field; for the pastures of the wilderness do spring, for the tree beareth her fruit, the fig tree and the vine do yield their strength." In other words, "You may not have anything to eat for a little while, but something dramatic is going to happen—the pastures of the wilderness are going to spring forth, and there's going to be a proliferation of crops" (cf. Isa. 30:23-24; 35:1-2, 6-7). Marvelous things are going to happen in the kingdom when the Lord puts the land back together.

   Continuing on in verse 23: "Be glad then, ye children of Zion, and rejoice in the Lord, your God; for he hath given you the former rain moderately, and he will cause to come down for you the rain, the former rain and the latter rain in the first month." People make a big issue out of the significance of "the former rain and the latter rain," but it simply refers to the autumn rains and the spring rains that secured the crops in the land of Israel. In other words, there is going to be so much rain when the kingdom begins that everything is going to experience incredible growth. God's going to cause a normal season of rain to fall in the first month of the kingdom to

40

make everything grow—so much so that "the floors shall be full of wheat, and the vats shall overflow with wine and oil. And I will restore to you the years that the locust hath eaten, the cankerworm, and the caterpillar, and the palmer worm, my great army which I sent among you" (vv. 24-25). All the crops that were lost during the Tribulation will be proliferating in the restoration.

Verses 26-27 say, "Ye shall eat in plenty, and be satisfied, and praise the name of the Lord, your God, who hath dealt wondrously with you; and my people shall never be ashamed. And ye shall know that I am in the midst of Israel, and that I am the Lord, your God, and none else; and my people shall never be ashamed." When will the Lord be in the midst of Israel? When Christ sits on His throne in the city of David and reigns during the millennial kingdom.

The context of Joel 2 is the great millennial kingdom, when the Jews are in their land, when the crops begin to grow, when the desert blossoms like a rose, when it rains in the first month as it would rain in a whole year of rain, when everything grows without the threat of pestilence or plague, and when everybody worships and praises God. That has never happened in the history of Israel; it's referring to the kingdom.

3. The Spirit's work in the kingdom (vv. 28-29)

Look at verses 28-29: "It shall come to pass afterward [after the kingdom has begun], that I will pour out my Spirit upon all flesh; and your sons and your daughters shall prophesy, your old men shall dream dreams, your young men shall see visions; and, also, upon the servants and upon the handmaids in those days will I pour out my Spirit."

4. The signs preceding the kingdom (vv. 30-31)

To further clarify when "those days" of verses 28-29 occur, verses 30-31 tell us, "I will show wonders in the heavens and in the earth: blood, and fire, and pillars of smoke. The sun shall be turned into darkness, and the moon into blood, before the great and the terrible day of the Lord come." In other words, all of these signs will follow the great judgment, and then the kingdom will be set up.

You don't have to be a Hebrew scholar to see what Joel 2:28-29 is talking about. The word *afterward* is the key. It tells us that the Spirit will be poured out after the army of the north has been defeated, after the day of the Lord with all the signs and wonders has occurred, and after the kingdom has been set up.

B. The Comparative Passages

1. Ezekiel 36:24-27

Referring to what will happen in the kingdom, Ezekiel quotes God as saying, "I will take you from among the nations, and gather you out of all countries, and will bring you into your own land. Then will I sprinkle clean water upon you, and ye shall be clean; from all your filthiness, and from all your idols, will I cleanse you. A new heart also will I give you, and a new spirit will I put within you; and I will take away the stony heart out of your flesh, and I will give you an heart of flesh. And I will put my Spirit within you, and cause you to walk in my statutes, and ye shall keep mine ordinances, and do them."

Can "the Former Rain and the Latter Rain" of Joel 2:23 Be Taken Metaphorically?

There is no basis for believing that Joel 2 has anything to do with the present. Some people say that "the former rain" refers to the speaking in tongues that occurred in Acts 2 on the Day of Pentecost, and that "the latter rain" refers to the speaking in tongues that is occurring now. First of all, the rain in Joel 2:23 is nothing more than plain water. The context has nothing to do with speaking in tongues.

If there is a metaphor in that verse at all, the metaphor is this: the former rain could be referring to David's kingdom and the latter rain is the Messiah's kingdom. That would be the only possible pic-

42

ture that Joel could be making. In other words, "David's kingdom was nice, but it had its problems. The Messiah's kingdom, however, is going to be far superior." The context of the passage is clearly the millennial kingdom.

Can the Current Charismatic Movement Be Supported Biblically?

There is nothing in Scripture to support the current charismatic movement. Nothing in the Bible substantiates the notion that God would do now what He did in the apostolic age in reference to the gift of languages. People who want to claim that this is the age of the outpouring of the Spirit have no biblical support. The only thing the Bible says about that particular time is in reference to Israel; and God's Spirit hasn't been poured out on Israel as a whole yet. Right now there's only a remnant of believing Jews. The outpouring of the Spirit referred to in Joel 2:28-29 will not occur until the Tribulation is over, until the second coming is over, and until Jesus sets up His kingdom and reigns in Jerusalem. And when the Spirit is poured out, He will be poured out on all flesh.

Furthermore, Joel 2:28-29 doesn't say anything about anyone's speaking in tongues. It does talk about prophecy, dreams, and visions—but it does not talk about tongues. Why? Because when tongues ceased, they ceased permanently. That's the meaning of the Greek word for "cease" (*pauō*) in 1 Corinthians 13:8. The gift of tongues has ceased—never to return.

2. Acts 2:16-21

If Joel 2 isn't referring to the gift of tongues, why does Peter quote it on the Day of Pentecost? Because there is so much confusion on this point, let's examine Acts 2.

a) The announcement

Peter explained the miraculous witness he and the other apostles made in many different languages by saying, "This is that which was spoken through the prophet, Joel: And it shall come to pass in the last days, saith God, I will pour out of my Spirit upon all flesh; and your sons and your daughters shall proph-

43

esy" (vv. 16-17*a*). Some conclude Peter identified what happened at Pentecost as the outpouring of the Spirit discussed in Joel. However, look at verses 19-20. Did the following events occur on the Day of Pentecost? "I will show wonders in heaven above, and signs in the earth beneath: blood, and fire, and vapor of smoke. The sun shall be turned into darkness, and the moon into blood, before that great and notable day of the Lord come." Did all that happen? No. It is in the future. Peter's quoting Joel, who was talking about the coming of the kingdom.

b) The application

Why did Peter quote something about the kingdom on the Day of Pentecost? I believe he was simply telling the people that the power they had seen displayed was a preliminary glimpse of the kind of power that the Spirit would release over all flesh in the kingdom. What the crowd in Jerusalem saw happen was a sign of what God's Spirit would someday do on a worldwide basis. In other words, it was a glimpse of the kingdom. The writer of Hebrews alludes to this when he refers to the tasting of "the powers of the age to come" (Heb. 6:5). The Jews who were present at Pentecost received a taste of the kind of power that will be released in the kingdom when Christ comes during the great and terrible day of the Lord.

One of the great biblical scholars of the nineteenth century, George N. H. Peters, wrote, "The Baptism of Pentecost is a pledge of fulfillment in the future, evidencing what the Holy Ghost will yet perform in the coming age" (*The Theocratic Kingdom* [Grand Rapids: Kregel, 1972], p. 66). German theologian Helmut Thielicke holds the same view. He considers the miracles of the first century as "the lightning of the Kingdom of God on the horizon" (*Man in God's World* [New York: Harper and Row, 1963], p. 112). He's right. Those first-century miracles were the lightning flashes that were to draw attention beyond the horizon to the coming millennial kingdom. That's exactly

44

what happened at Pentecost. It was not the fulfillment of Joel's prophecy. That is yet to be fulfilled in the kingdom.

Summarizing what we've seen, Joel 2:28-29 can't be used as a basis for saying that the gift of tongues has started up again for the following reasons: Joel did not say that tongues would accompany the outpouring of the Spirit, and the outpouring of the Spirit at Pentecost was not the outpouring that Joel prophesied. Joel's prophecy was in reference to the millennial kingdom. What happened at Pentecost was simply a glimpse of the power that will occur in the kingdom.

The whole point of Paul's argument in 1 Corinthians 13:8 is that tongues will cease. There's nothing in the Bible that supports the belief that tongues will return in the church age. You can search throughout the Bible, but you will not find the gift of tongues starting again. Some people say, "What about Luke 11:13, where Jesus says He'll 'give the Holy Spirit to them that ask him'? We're asking for the Spirit and the gift of tongues, and He's giving them to us." People may be asking for the gift of tongues, but if God isn't giving that gift in this particular age, those people may be receiving something that isn't from God.

III. AN EXPLANATION OF THE CURRENT TONGUES PHENOMENON

You may say, "If I accept the fact that the gift of tongues has ceased, and what's going on today isn't scriptural, what is going on? How do you explain all the people who are apparently speaking in tongues?" Let me suggest some answers.

A. Some Realistic Possibilities

   1. Demonic influences

      Every false religion in the world was spawned from the same individual—Satan. The Old Testament says that "all the gods of the nations are idols [lit., "demons"]" (Ps. 96:5a). There's demonic influence behind every false religious system. Whenever tongues occur in a false religion, it's highly possible that its basic source is Satan or demons.

Joseph Dillow, in his book *Speaking in Tongues*, has compiled the following data, complete with references: "The *Encyclopaedia Brittanica* cites many instances of tongues speaking in pagan cults. . . . D. C. Graham tells of a girl in the Szechwan province of China who was possessed by demons and 'began to utter words incoherently.' Edward Langston says that in East Africa many persons possessed by demons speak fluently in Swahili or English, although under normal circumstances they do not understand either language. Junod reports that among the Thonga people of Africa, when a demon is being exorcised the person sings a curative song which he himself composes. Usually the songs are in the Zulu tongue. Even if the person does not know this language it is claimed that he will be able to use it 'by a kind of miracle of tongues.' As far back as Virgil (70-19 B.C.) there are references to the tongues speaking of the Sibylline priestess on the Isle of Delos. This is described in his *Aeneid*. Today, ecstatic speech is found among the Muslims, and the Eskimos of Greenland. Non-Christian alchemists of the middle ages were reported to have spoken in tongues. This caused them to be popularly feared as men skilled in sorcery. The Bwiti cult among the Fang people of the Gabon Republic has been observed speaking in tongues. The parapsychology laboratory of the University of Virginia Medical School reports incidents of occult speaking in tongues. A Turkish actress claims she learns the 'language of Jakosta' from a black man she sees in her dreams. Joseph Smith, the founder of the non-Christian sect of Mormonism taught his followers to speak in tongues in the following manner, 'Arise upon your feet, speak or make some sound, continue to make sounds of some kind, and the Lord will make a tongue or language of it' " (*Speaking in Tongues* [Grand Rapids: Zondervan, 1975], pp. 172-73).

There are all kinds of possibilities for Satan and his demons to introduce this phenomenon of speaking in
tongues. To say that the existence of speaking in
tongues validates the practice as being from God is foolish—as foolish as saying that the existence of a religion
proves it's of God.

2. Learned behavior

For the most part speaking in tongues is not a supernatural or miraculous experience. It is simply something
that a person learns how to do. I believe that this is the
most common explanation for what is happening today.
People are learning how to speak in tongues. One of the
reasons I say that is the amazing similarity in the terms
that I have heard used by tongues speakers all over the
country. They all speak the same thing in the same way.
In fact, I've heard the same things spoken so many
times, that I could repeat those words and "speak in
tongues" myself. The claim, however, that is constantly
made by charismatics is that every Christian is supposed to receive his own private prayer language.

John Kildahl, in his book *The Psychology of Speaking in
Tongues* (New York: Harper and Row, 1972), says that
speaking in tongues is a learned behavior. Commis-
sioned by the American Lutheran church and the Na-
tional Institute of Mental Health to do a long-range
study on the phenomenon of tongues, John Kildahl (a
clinical psychologist) and Paul Qualben (a psychiatrist)
concluded that the vast majority of tongues speaking
was simply learned behavior. People learn how to speak
in tongues because they are told that it is the right thing
to do.

a) The deliberate inducement of tongues

I went to a meeting of the Children of God cult one
night to help persuade someone to get out from under their influences and to see what was going on
there for myself. As I was sitting in the lobby, I was
able to listen to someone as he tried to teach a new

47

convert to speak in tongues. In a most laborious way, he tried to induce this man to receive the gift of tongues. Even though he tried to give him all the steps and procedures to speak in tongues, the man couldn't figure out what to do. On another occasion I was watching a charismatic talk show on television. When the person being interviewed confessed to having spiritual problems, the interviewer said, "Have you spoken in tongues and used your prayer language every day?" "No, I haven't," the person admitted. "That's your problem, then," replied the interviewer. "You have to do that every day. And it doesn't matter how it starts; because once you get it started the Holy Spirit will keep it going." When I heard that, I thought, *If the Holy Spirit wants them to speak in tongues so much, why doesn't He start it going Himself?* It doesn't make sense. Furthermore, it is intimidating for someone to say, "Your spiritual problems stem from the fact that you aren't speaking in tongues."

b) The disillusioning potential of tongues

When speaking in tongues is a learned behavior and strongly induced by pressure from someone else, it is a potential for great disillusionment. Why? Because once the experience comes, people eventually realize that it is nothing more than learned behavior. They also realize that it isn't supernatural and that it doesn't do what people say it will do. People end up having the same problems in their lives whether they speak in tongues or not, so they become disillusioned. According to Kildahl and Qualben, the more sincere a person is when he starts to speak in tongues, the more disillusioned he can become.

Kildahl and Qualben also point out that peer pressure and the desire to belong cause a strong sense of identification and attachment to a certain leader or group. However, when people lose confidence in either the group or the leader, these people cease speaking in tongues.

3. Psychological persuasion

Some of the more bizarre cases of tongues speaking may have a psychological explanation.

a) Motor automatism

Have you ever watched a newscast that showed teenage girls at a rock concert screaming over a musician? In the heat of the excitement, emotion, fervor, and loud noise, people sometimes lose voluntary control of their vocal chords and their muscles. Sometimes they even fall to the ground in convulsions. Why? Because the brain has tremendous control over the body—including speech. Psychologically, then, tongues can be explained as motor automatism, which is clinically described as "radical inward detachment from one's conscious surroundings."

Motor automatism is a disassociation of nearly all voluntary muscles from conscious control. Some call it ecstasy, which is described as "a pleasurable state of intense emotion linked with an altered state of consciousness." We've all experienced moments when we have felt detached, woozy, and a little faint. With the right kind of driving, pounding emotion, coupled with the kind of rhythmical music that is often associated with charismatic gatherings, a person could easily lose conscious control and be driven to speak in tongues.

b) Hypnosis

Psychologically, tongues can also be explained by group hypnosis, individual hypnosis, or self-hypnosis. Kildahl and Qualben made the statement that "hypnotizability constitutes the *sine qua non* of the glossolalia experience" (p. 54). They also concluded that people who fall into the tongues movement are usually the kind who are hypnotizable. Not everyone is hypnotizable. According to Kildahl and Qualben, people who are submissive, easily influenced, and dependent on a leader are the types who fall into speaking in tongues. When people's desire to belong is strong enough, they become more submissive to the power of suggestion. Then when emotion runs high and the pressure becomes great, tongues can result.

We can't go around trying to determine the specific reason for each person's tongues experience. The only reason I'm mentioning these things is to show you that there are many explanations for speaking in tongues other than the explanation that it's of the Holy Spirit. In fact, we know the Holy Spirit can't be responsible for what's going on today because the Bible says that the gift of tongues has ceased.

Dr. E. Mansell Pattison, a member of the Christian Association for Psychological Studies and an instructor at the University of Washington School of Medicine, made the following observation: "The product of our analysis is the demonstration of the very natural mechanisms that produce glossolalia. As a psychological phenomenon, glossolalia is easy to produce and readily understandable. I can add my own observations from clinical experiences with neurological and psychiatric patients. In certain types of brain disorders resulting from strokes, brain tumors, etc., the patient is left with disruptions in his automatic physical speech circuit patterns. If we study these 'aphasic' patients we can observe the same decomposition of speech that occurs in glossolalia. Similar decomposition of speech occurs in schizophrenic thought and speech patterns, which are structurally the same as glossolalia. This data can be understood to demonstrate that the same stereotypes of speech will result whenever conscious, willful control of speech is interfered with, whether by injury to the brain, by psychosis, or by passive renunciation of willful control."

Entering a state of "passive renunciation of willful control" is essentially what is recommended to those who want to speak in tongues. People are told to release themselves, to give up the control of their voices, to just say words and let them flow without thinking about what's being said. Dr. Pattison continues, "This corroborates our previous assessment that glossolalia is a stereotyped pattern of unconsciously controlled vocal behavior which appears under specific emotional conditions" ("Speaking in Tongues and About Tongues," *Christian Standard* [15 February 1964]: 2).

Dr. Pattison's conclusion, then, is that glossolalia (tongues) can occur wherever conscious, willful control of the brain is interfered with—which could either be psychological or physiological.

B. Some Reasons for Its Popularity

1. A deep spiritual hunger

Basically, I believe that the popularity of tongues comes from a deep spiritual hunger. People are told that speaking in tongues is a great spiritual experience and if they haven't done it they haven't succeeded spiritually. Since they haven't been properly taught the Bible, they believe they need this experience.

2. A need for spiritual expression

People are seeking for some way to express themselves spiritually because many of them have been attending church for years without any real involvement.

3. A craving for instant spirituality

Within the charismatic movement, speaking in tongues is considered to be a manifestation of spirituality or holiness; therefore it attracts those who desire that external recognition.

4. A reaction to society

Another reason for the popularity of tongues is that it is a reaction to our secularized, mechanized, academic, cold, indifferent society. Speaking in tongues gives a person the feeling that he's involved in something supernatural rather than academic and explicable in terms of reason.

5. A need for acceptance and security

The need to belong, to be accepted, and to be secure drives people into movements where they can be a part of the group—where they can be among the ones who "have it." That can be satisfying. In fact, it's a form of self-actualization to be able to say, "I am a charismatic." It makes many people believe that they are something, belong to something, and have something that others don't have.

IV. AN EXHORTATION TO BE CHARACTERIZED BY LOVE

First Corinthians 13:8 tells us that tongues have ceased, but the point of the chapter is that love is eternal. We must never forget that. In discussing this whole issue of tongues I am trying to teach what the Word of God says. I don't have an ax to grind with charismatics—some of my friends are in that movement. In fact, I thank God for Pentecostal and charismatic people who believe in the authority of the Word of God. I believe they ought to study it a little more carefully, but I thank God that they believe it and hold it up as authoritative. I also thank God that they believe in the deity of Jesus Christ, His sacrificial death, His physical resurrection, salvation by faith and not works, the need to live a life of obedience, and to proclaim their faith. I thank God for all those things. I'm sorry we can't agree on this one issue, but they're still my brothers and sisters in Christ, and I'm commanded to love them. Remember, love is eternal, and the gifts are merely temporary.

I fear that people will try to shove this particular lesson about tongues down the throats of their charismatic friends. That's the last thing I want people to do! If you know Christians who are involved in this movement, the best thing to do is to constantly and fervently show them love so that they will disassociate love from speaking in tongues. That's important to do because they're under the false impression that Christians don't really know how to love until they've had the experience of speaking in tongues. I've heard charismatics say, "I never really loved until I had this experience. I've never felt so good or had such joy." If you show them that you have love, joy, and happiness, they may begin to see that those things aren't connected to tongues. Then, when the day comes that they ask you why you don't speak in tongues, you will have earned the right to show them.

It grieves my heart that there's a rift in the church over this issue. And I don't believe there's any point in forcing arguments —because that will make people harder to reach. What we need to do is to love charismatic Christians with all our hearts and be available to answer their questions when they ask. We also need to be sensitive for the right moment to come when we can tell them the truth in love. Remember, it's important that we love. That's the whole message of 1 Corinthians 13.

Is It Unloving to Criticize the Charismatic Movement?

I am constantly accused of being unloving because of my stand against speaking in tongues. But what is the definition of love? Is it unloving to speak the truth? Is it unloving to teach the Word of God? I love God and His Word more than I love anything else, so I'm going to proclaim His Word with boldness—even if it seems that I'm being unloving to people in the process. The Bible clearly says that we are to be "speaking the truth in love" (Eph. 4:15a)— and that's exactly what I'm doing.

I know that I'm not always right. But I don't stand alone in what I teach about tongues. There are many, many scholars far more competent than I am who stand on the same ground. I'm confident that the Word of God teaches that the gift of tongues has ceased. And because I believe that is the truth, the most loving thing I can do is to teach it. When people know the truth, they're able to live it out and be in the place of God's blessing.

People sometimes say, "You shouldn't get into controversial subjects. When there's an issue like that in the text you should not deal with it." That's the worst thing I could do! Should I ignore God's Word? Am I doing anyone a favor by not telling him the truth? Of course not. If I'm in error, I pray that someone will show me where I'm wrong. But I believe that what I've said is the truth of the Word of God, so I have to deal with it as such. And I hope you sense that I'm speaking in love.

Focusing on the Facts

1. Love is not a _____ or an _____; it is a spirit of _____ (see p. 35).
2. Christians should be recognized by what dominant characteristic? Support your answer from Scripture (see p. 35).
3. In discussing the issue of speaking in tongues, what attitude is essential to maintain? Why (see p. 36)?
4. What is the world's definition of love? Why is it important for the world to see Christians demonstrate love to one another (see p. 36)?
5. Does loving one another as Christians mean we are to avoid controversial subjects? Explain (see p. 36).
6. What are the two basic, overall reasons supporting the fact that tongues ceased in the apostolic age (see p. 38)?
7. When charismatics are presented with the evidence that the gift of tongues has ceased, they usually respond in one of two ways. What are these responses and their inherent problems (see pp. 38-39)?
8. What Old Testament passage is used by charismatics to support the belief that tongues may have stopped in the apostolic age but have started up again in this last century? Why can't that passage be legitimately used to support this belief (see pp. 39-45)?
9. What time in history is indicated in the context of Joel 2:20-31? What is the meaning of the word *afterward* in Joel 2:28? Why is it significant (see pp. 39-42)?
10. How do charismatics translate the phrase "the former rain and the latter rain" in Joel 2:23? If this phrase can be taken metaphorically, what is the only possible interpretation that can be taken and still be fair to the context (see pp. 40-43)?
11. Does Joel 2:28-29 make reference to the gift of tongues returning in the kingdom? Why or why not (see p. 43)?
12. Why does Peter quote Joel 2:28-32 on the Day of Pentecost in Acts 2:16-20 (see pp. 43-45)?
13. What indications do we have that some of the tongues speaking that occurs is demonically induced (see pp. 45-46)?
14. Why is it foolish to argue that the mere existence of tongues validates it as being from God (see p. 47)?

15. What is probably the most common explanation for the speaking in tongues that is going on in the modern charismatic movement? What is the evidence that supports this (see pp. 47-48)?
16. Why does speaking in tongues create such a great potential for disillusionment? What relationship does the person's level of sincerity have to the possible degree of disillusionment (see p. 48)?
17. What is the probable explanation for the most bizarre cases of speaking in tongues (see p. 49)?
18. What is motor automatism? What kind of environment creates this psychological state? How does this relate to speaking in tongues (see p. 49)?
19. What factors make up the hypnotizability of a person? What role does this hypnotizability play in a person's susceptibility to falling into the practice of speaking in tongues (see pp. 49-50)?
20. There are many explanations for the phenomenon of speaking in tongues. How do we know that one of the explanations is not the Holy Spirit (see p. 50)?
21. Based on the observations made in his clinical experience with neurological and psychiatric patients, what conclusion did Dr. E. Mansell Pattison make regarding tongues (see pp. 50-51)?
22. What are some of the reasons for the current popularity of speaking in tongues (see pp. 51-52)?
23. What is the most effective way to reach people in the charismatic movement with biblical truth about the issue of tongues? Why (see pp. 52-53)?
24. Is it unloving to criticize the practice of speaking in tongues? Explain (see p. 53).

Pondering the Principles

1. Look up the following verses: John 13:35; 1 John 2:9-10; 3:16, 18. Then answer the following questions: How is the world going to recognize that you are a Christian? What conclusions can be made about your life if you hate your brother? What is the ultimate sacrifice you should be willing to make for another Christian? Is it adequate to simply tell someone that you love him?

What must accompany your words? Why? Read over these verses again and evaluate your own love life.

2. If you are not a charismatic or Pentecostal believer, how do you respond to charismatic Christians? Do you fellowship with them and have relationships based on mutual love for one another and for the Lord Jesus Christ? If you don't, why not? Is it simply because you don't come in contact with charismatic Christians or because you avoid contact with them? Biblically, what is your response to be? If you are a charismatic, how do you respond to Christians who don't believe that speaking in tongues is a current manifestation of the Holy Spirit? Do you see them as second-class Christians or Christians in need of something more? Do you try to force your experience on them through intimidation? All Christians—whether charismatic or not—are to love their brothers and sisters in Christ. But remember, this does not mean you are to ignore the truth of God's Word. First John 3:18 says we are to love "in deed and in truth."

3

The Permanence of Love—Part 3

Outline

Introduction

Review
I. The Prominence of Love (vv. 1-3)
II. The Perfections of Love (vv. 4-7)
III. The Permanence of Love (vv. 8-12)
   A. Gifts Are Temporary—Love Is Eternal (v. 8)

Lesson
   B. Gifts Are Partial—Love Is Complete (vv. 9-10, 12)
      1. The confines of prophecy and knowledge (v. 9)
         a) The lack of completeness
           (1) Prophecy is partial
           (2) Knowledge is partial
         b) The level of competency
           (1) 2 Peter 1:3*a*
           (2) 1 John 5:20*a*
           (3) 1 Corinthians 2:12
         c) The logic of concealment
           (1) The capacity of our minds
           (2) The corruption of our minds
      2. The clarification of "that which is perfect" (vv. 10, 12)
         a) The present vagueness
         b) The predominant views
           (1) The completion of Scripture
           (2) The rapture of the church
           (3) The maturity of the church
           (4) The second coming
           (5) The eternal state
   C. Gifts Are Elementary—Love Is Mature (v. 11)

IV. The Preeminence of Love (v. 13)

Introduction

We have been studying the thirteenth chapter of 1 Corinthians—a chapter about love. The great climax of this chapter begins in verse 8 with the phrase "love never faileth." In other words, love is the only thing that is eternal—the only link we have with eternity. The Corinthians had emphasized spiritual gifts, ministries, and other good things, but they had forgotten what was best. They had forgotten what Paul calls in 1 Corinthians 12:31 the "more excellent way"—love. Paul writes chapter 13 and makes a major statement on the essence, character, and quality of love.

Review

I. THE PROMINENCE OF LOVE (vv. 1-3)

II. THE PERFECTIONS OF LOVE (vv. 4-7)

III. THE PERMANENCE OF LOVE (vv. 8-12)

A. Gifts Are Temporary—Love Is Eternal (v. 8; pp. 14-19, 37)

"Love never faileth; but whether there be prophecies, they shall be done away [lit., "be rendered inoperative, abolished, done away"]; whether there be tongues, they shall cease [lit., "stop by themselves"]; whether there be knowledge, it shall vanish away [lit., "be rendered inoperative, abolished, done away"]."

Paul used these three gifts—prophecy, tongues, and knowledge—as a composite of all the gifts. The most significant gift was prophecy, the least significant gift was tongues, and the gift representative of the middle would be knowledge. Paul was simply saying, "Gifts are a passing reality; they are not forever. They have their time and their place, but they are not permanent or eternal."

In previous lessons we discussed the distinction that Paul made between the gifts of prophecy and knowledge and the gift of tongues. We saw that he used the verb *pauō* in the middle voice, which says that tongues will stop by themselves. The verb he used for prophecy and knowledge (*katargeō*) is in the passive voice and means that something will stop those gifts, halt them, bring them to an end. And what is it that stops those two gifts? Verse 10 describes it as "that which is perfect."

Prophecy and knowledge didn't cease with tongues; they continued on and are now waiting for that perfect thing to stop them. Verses 9-10 say, "We know in part, and we prophesy in part. But when that which is perfect is come, then that which is in part shall be done away." The partial things—knowledge and prophecy—are going to stop when the perfect thing comes, because they're only temporary. They are important—in fact, they're essential. But they're only part of time, not eternity.

Lesson

B. Gifts Are Partial—Love Is Complete (vv. 9-10, 12)

If you look at verses 9, 10, and 12, you'll see that the phrase "in part" is used four times. Paul uses the Greek word *meros*, which simply means "a part of the whole." The gifts, then, are partial. By the way, it's interesting to notice that tongues do not appear in verses 9-13. Why? Because they have stopped. In Paul's illustration here in 1 Corinthians 13, the only things that will be around when the perfect thing comes are prophecy and knowledge. There will be other gifts, of course, but the representative gifts that Paul refers to here are prophecy and knowledge. By the time the perfect thing comes, tongues will have already stopped by themselves.

1. The confines of prophecy and knowledge (v. 9)

    "For we know in part, and we prophesy in part."

    a) The lack of completeness

(1) Prophecy is partial

I may study diligently and do everything I can to preach the Word of God, but at best I can preach only a part of all the truths of God. Why? Because I'm limited to my own understanding of what God has revealed, and I'm limited by the fact that a human mind cannot understand a superhuman God in His fullness. At best, preaching (or prophesying, which literally means "to speak before") is partial.

(2) Knowledge is partial

The gift of knowledge, which is the Spirit-given ability to draw principles out of the Word of God, is only partial. There is no way we can know everything there is to know. I thought I knew everything when I graduated from seminary! But I've been losing that attitude along the way. No Christian can have perfect knowledge.

(a) 1 Corinthians 8:2—"If any man think that he knoweth anything, he knoweth nothing yet as he ought to know." Knowledge is limited. In fact, if you think you know everything, you actually know very little. Why? Because as Socrates said, the basis of knowledge is realizing that you can't know everything.

(b) Job 11:7-8—"Canst thou by searching find out God? Canst thou find out the Almighty unto perfection? It is as high as heaven; what canst thou do? Deeper than sheol; what canst thou know?" In other words, it's impossible to attain the fullness of the knowledge of God. You can't climb high enough or descend low enough. It's beyond the capacity of man to fully understand God.

People often ask why Bible teachers or other mature Christians disagree. It's because all of us are dealing with limited knowledge. We're trying to put all the pieces together and make conclusions without full knowledge.

(c) Job 26:14—After talking about God and how marvelous and powerful He is, Job exclaimed, "Lo, these are parts of his ways; but how little a portion is heard of him! But the thunder of his power, who can understand?" It's beyond all of us to grasp the fullness of God's power, God's ways, God's truth, and God's nature.

(d) Psalm 40:5—"Many, O Lord, my God, are thy wonderful works which thou hast done, and thy thoughts which are toward us; they cannot be reckoned up in order unto thee." In other words, David said, "When I try to catalog and systematize them and offer them back to You, there's something missing." Then he said, "If I would declare and speak of them, they are more than can be numbered." Systematizing God is difficult because we don't have all the necessary information.

(e) Psalm 139:6—"Such knowledge is too wonderful for me; it is high, I cannot attain unto it." The knowledge of God is far beyond us.

(f) Romans 11:33-34—"Oh, the depth of the riches both of the wisdom and knowledge of God! How unsearchable are his judgments, and his ways past finding out! For who hath known the mind of the Lord? Or who hath been his counselor?"

(g) Colossians 2:3—You say, "But when you know Christ, don't you receive it all?" No, because in Him alone "are hidden all the treasures of wisdom and knowledge." To know Christ is to know that wisdom and knowledge are hidden in Him. Not everything has been revealed.

b) The level of competency

We have to remember that we're always dealing with a part of the truth in terms of its total. But I want to hasten to say that just because we have partial truth does not mean we have error. It simply means that we don't have all the truth there is. For example, you might teach your child that two plus two is four. If you do, you have taught him truth. However, that's a long way from algebra, geometry, trigonometry, and calculus. Even if your child is able to apprehend the fact that two plus two equals four, there is so much more to know that your child would not be able to understand. In a similar way the knowledge that we have is not wrong or unreliable; it is simply incomplete. As we grow as Christians, we continually learn more and more—but we won't receive it all. Yet even though our knowledge is partial, we have all that we need.

(1) 2 Peter 1:3*a*—Peter said that God "hath given unto us all things that pertain unto life and godliness." In other words, we have all we need.

(2) 1 John 5:20*a*—The apostle John said, "We know that the Son of God is come, and hath given us an understanding, that we may know him that is true."

(3) 1 Corinthians 2:12—Paul said that "we have received . . . the Spirit who is of God; that we might know the things that are freely given to us of God."

We know as much as we need to know of what God wants us to do. But we don't know everything. We're just a bunch of students trying to grasp the basics.

c) The logic of concealment

Why didn't God give us all the knowledge there is to know? I believe there are two reasons.

(1) The capacity of our minds

> The human mind would never be able to understand all of God's truths; therefore God limited what He gave us and kept it simple. The gospel is so simple, in fact, that a child can understand it.

(2) The corruption of our minds

> A sin-defiled, depraved human mind can't deal with ultimate truth in its fullness. Someday when we get a perfect mind, we'll get all truth. But that is in the future.

We have partial knowledge. Some of it comes through the gift of preaching as men declare to us the Word of God, and some of it comes as men draw out principles in Scripture and teach them to us. These are, in part, contributing to what we know.

2. The clarification of "that which is perfect" (vv. 10, 12)

"But when that which is perfect is come, then that which is in part shall be done away [Gk., *katargeō*, "abolished, rendered inoperative"]. . . . For now we see in a mirror, darkly; but then, face to face; now I know in part, but then shall I know even as also I am known."

There's coming a day when we won't need books, sermons, classes, or Bible studies. We won't need any of those things because we'll know it all. In fact, there won't even be a need for any of the gifts. However, one thing will remain—love. That's Paul's whole point. Love will remain throughout eternity.

a) The present vagueness

> Verse 12 says, "For now we see in a mirror, darkly." That's referring to prophecy. We can perceive what God is doing, we can perceive His Word, and we can

perceive His program—but only partially. Someday, however, we will be face to face with God and have full perception. Further, referring to the gift of knowledge, Paul said, "Now I know in part, but then shall I know even as also I am known."

The illustration of seeing in a mirror darkly was appropriate to use with the Corinthians. They would know exactly what Paul was talking about because one of the trades in the city of Corinth was mirror making. In those days they made mirrors by flattening out a piece of metal and polishing it to a high shine. If you've ever looked into a metal mirror, however, you know that it tends to be a little wavy, which somewhat distorts the image. Additionally, after a period of time, metal mirrors are prone to decay —becoming blotched and marred. Paul was saying, "For now, we are looking in a mirror that reveals a rather vague and confined image."

When you look in a car's rearview mirror while you're driving, the information available to you is limited by the small size of that mirror. Have you ever looked in your rearview mirror as you began to change lanes, only to be startled by a loud honk from a car that you hadn't seen? You hadn't seen the car because it was in your blind spot. That's essentially what Paul is saying in verse 12. There is a vagueness, a dimness in what we see. There are limitations to what we see in terms of preaching and teaching the Word of God. Our knowledge is limited as well. But there's coming a day when we will be able to see the real picture without a mirror—face to face. The time will come when we will know, without any limitations, the fullness of knowledge. That's a fantastic promise. Just imagine the day when we will know everything and see everything the way it really is.

b) The predominant views

(1) The completion of Scripture

Some people say "that which is perfect" is the completion of Scripture and has, therefore, already come. That is a popular view today. It is believed that when the completed New Testament was added to the Old Testament, the perfect thing had arrived. This view also says that Scripture causes us to see face to face and to know as we are known. I believe this view is weak for the following reasons.

(a) This view would have been obscure to the Corinthians. Remember, Paul was basically writing to a group of people to present a message to them that they would understand. In a sense we are eavesdropping on Paul's correspondence with the Corinthians. I don't believe that the Corinthians would have comprehended the word *perfect* in that way. For one thing, the New Testament was not yet complete when 1 Corinthians was written. In Matthew 5:48 Jesus says, "Be ye, therefore, perfect, even as your Father, who is in heaven, is perfect." That was written before 1 Corinthians. In the mind of the Corinthians, then, where would perfection be? In heaven. Jesus was setting the ultimate standard of absolute holiness. Perfection is always the highest level of attainment. It's likely that the Corinthians would have seen perfection in terms of being like Christ or like God—fully matured.

(b) This view requires prophecy and knowledge (which are primarily related to proclaiming and teaching the Word of God) to cease upon the completion of the canon. Basically, this view eliminates the manifestations of those gifts. While Scripture was being written, the writers of Scripture were preaching from passages that were already written. The gift of prophecy was revelatory as well as reiterating what had already been revealed. If "that

which is perfect" is the Bible, then the spiritual gifts of prophecy and knowledge would
have had to stop when the Bible was completed. For reasons we will soon discuss, it is difficult to believe that the gifts of proclaiming
and drawing truths out of Scripture stopped
once Scripture was completed.

(c) This view forces the conclusion that there is
no proclaiming or teaching throughout the
entire church age, Tribulation, and kingdom.
This is difficult to believe because Joel 2:28
says that there will be prophecy in the kingdom, and Revelation 11:3 refers to two prophets that God raises up during the Tribulation.
If there is prophecy in the Tribulation and in
the millennial kingdom, then prophecy cannot have ceased. There is still yet a future for
prophecy, to say nothing of the proclaiming
and teaching going on throughout the church
age.

Those who hold to this view say, "The gifts of
prophecy and knowledge stop and then start
up again." But that can't be true for two reasons. First, the verb used in 1 Corinthians
13:8 regarding the future of these gifts means
"to be abolished." Second, if these gifts start
up again, Paul's whole point in 1 Corinthians
13 is destroyed. He was saying, "Some things
stop, and they're done, but love is forever."
His contrast was not, "Certain things come
and go, but love is forever." That's a weak
contrast. His point was a strong contrast:
"Some things stop, but love goes on forever."

(d) The phrase "face to face" can't be explained
by this view. You own a Bible, but have you
ever seen God face to face? No. In fact, we
haven't even seen the One who reveals
God—the Lord Jesus Christ. First Peter 1:8
says, "Whom, having not seen, ye love."
Having a Bible doesn't mean that we've seen
God face to face. Someday that will happen

—when we go to heaven and when God's glory fills the new heaven and the new earth and shines out of the midst of the Holy City. Then we'll see His glory face to face, but that hasn't happened yet.

(e) The phrase "then shall I know even as also I am known" is not explained by this view. Do I know God as well as God knows me because I have a Bible? No. God knows me perfectly, but I know Him only in part. Even though I have a Bible, I don't know all there is to know about God. In John 10:15 Jesus says, "As the Father knoweth me, even so know I the Father." I can't say that. I don't know the Father in the same sense that He knows me. My knowledge of Him is limited.

To summarize, the view that Scripture is "that which is perfect" (v. 10) is weak for the following reasons: (1) it would have had an obscure meaning to the Corinthians, (2) it ends prophecy and knowledge long before the kingdom and the Tribulation, where they appear, (3) it can't explain "face to face," and (4) it can't explain "then shall I know even as also I am known."

(2) The rapture of the church

This is probably the most common interpretation of "that which is perfect." In fact, that is what I believed for many years. But I believe this view is also weak because, like the first view, it can't explain why prophecy and knowledge are going on in the Tribulation and the kingdom if they cease at the rapture. This view admits that prophecy and knowledge are present in the church age and in the kingdom, but it denies that they are present in the Tribulation. But if these gifts cease at the rapture, they can't start up again in the kingdom. Once they're abolished, they're abolished. Further, how does this view explain the prophesying of the two witnesses during the first three-and-a-half years of the Tribulation (Rev. 11:3)?

67

Incidentally, the word *perfect* (Gk., *to teleion*) in verse 10 is neuter. This is significant because any term that is used in reference to the rapture or the second coming is always feminine in the Greek. It's unlikely that the rapture is "that which is perfect." Otherwise the word would be in the feminine form.

(3) The maturity of the church

This view states that "that which is perfect" is when the church reaches its maturity—in other words, when the Body is complete. That is simply another way of identifying the rapture. Why? Because when the Body is complete the church will be raptured. What would the church do if it were complete and there weren't anyone left to win to Christ?

The basis of this view is the translation of *to teleion* to refer to maturity rather than perfection. However, it still has the same problem as the other views. For example, if prophecy and knowledge cease when the church is mature and taken out of the world, then how does one explain the existence of prophecy and knowledge in the Tribulation and the kingdom?

(4) The second coming

This view basically states that Christ, or His coming, is the perfect thing. The problem, however, is that *to teleion* is neuter. If it were referring to the second coming the word would be feminine, and if it were referring to Christ, it would be masculine. Christ isn't a thing. Christ is a *He*. Furthermore, if Christ comes and ends prophecy and knowledge, why is the kingdom filled with prophecy and knowledge? It doesn't make sense. There's going to be plenty of teaching and preaching in the kingdom.

Will There Be Preaching and Teaching in the Kingdom?

Let's see what Scripture has to say on this point.

1. Isaiah 11:9—If you read this entire chapter, it will be clear that it is describing the millennial kingdom. Verse 9 says, "They shall not hurt nor destroy in all my holy mountain; for the earth shall be full of the knowledge of the Lord, as the waters cover the sea." Somehow the entire world is going to be engulfed in knowledge, instruction, teaching, and preaching. It's going to dominate the kingdom.

2. Isaiah 12:3-4—Still speaking of the kingdom, Isaiah said, "Therefore, with joy shall ye draw water out of the wells of salvation." If there's going to be salvation in the kingdom, there's going to have to be proclamation in the kingdom as well, because you have to hear the message before you can believe it. Verse 4 continues, "In that day shall ye say, Praise the Lord, call upon his name, declare his doings among the people, make mention that his name is exalted." In other words, God is calling on Israel to preach and proclaim His name in the kingdom to bring people to salvation.

3. Isaiah 29:18—"In that day [the kingdom] shall the deaf hear the words of the book, and the eyes of the blind shall see out of obscurity, and out of darkness." In other words, there's going to be instruction in the kingdom. No longer will people be deaf and blind to it. Instruction will go on, and it will be carried out effectively.

4. Isaiah 30:20-21—"Though the Lord give you the bread of adversity, and the water of affliction, yet shall not thy teachers be removed into a corner any more, but thine eyes shall see thy teachers. And thine ears shall hear a word behind thee, saying, This is the way, walk ye in it, when ye turn to the right hand, and when ye turn to the left." In the kingdom there are going to be teachers all over the globe, and they're going to be saying, "Don't do that! Don't go that way; go this way." God is actually going to have emissaries all over the world directing people in the way they are to walk and in the way they are to go. There will be widespread instruction during the kingdom.

5. Isaiah 32:3-4—"The eyes of those who see shall not be dim, and the ears of those who hear shall hearken. The heart also of the rash shall understand knowledge, and the tongues of the stammerers shall be ready to speak plainly." There will be knowledge, understanding, and an apprehension of information and truth so that people will be led to righteous behavior as well as to salvation.

6. Isaiah 41:20—Verses 15-19 talk of the blessings of the kingdom, which will produce the following effect: "That they may see, and know, and consider, and understand together, that the hand of the Lord hath done this, and the Holy One of Israel hath created it." In the kingdom, information will be dispatched in order that people might know the truth about God.

7. Isaiah 2:2-3—"It shall come to pass in the last days, that the mountain of the Lord's house shall be established in the top of the mountains, and shall be exalted above the hills; and all nations shall flow unto it. And many people shall go and say, Come ye, and let us go up to the mountain of the Lord, to the house of the God of Jacob; and he will teach us of his ways, and we will walk in his paths; for out of Zion shall go forth the law, and the word of the Lord from Jerusalem." God's Word will literally proceed from Jerusalem to the world. There are going to be teachers all over the place, proclaiming and preaching the Word of God.

8. Isaiah 29:24b—In the kingdom "they that murmured shall learn doctrine." The kingdom will be filled with teachers and preachers.

9. Jeremiah 23:4a—After the Lord gathers His flock and brings them into His kingdom, He says, "I will set up shepherds over them who shall feed them." What does a spiritual shepherd do to feed his flock? He gives them the Word.

It is clear, then, that there will be teaching and preaching in the kingdom.

If there is going to be teaching and preaching in the kingdom, then those gifts haven't ceased. And if they haven't ceased yet, then "that which is perfect" has not yet come. That leaves us only one other possibility for the identity of that perfect thing.

(5) The eternal state

The eternal state—the new heaven and the new earth, which begin at the end of the millennial kingdom, fits all the requirements for the identity of "that which is perfect." What Paul is saying in 1 Corinthians 13 is, "You're going to need these spiritual gifts while you're existing in time, but love is all you'll need for eternity." It is a contrast between time and eternity.

(a) This view is the only view that allows for the neuter use of *to teleion* in verse 10. This verse refers to a perfect thing, not a person. And I believe the thing referred to is heaven (or the eternal state).

(b) This view is the only view that allows for prophecy and knowledge in the church age, the Tribulation, and the kingdom. One day when we go to heaven, we won't need preachers and teachers or Bible studies because we will be perfect as our Father in heaven is perfect.

(c) This is the only view that fits the context of 1 Corinthians 13. Paul was contrasting spiritual gifts with love by showing that the gifts exist only in time, but love will go on throughout eternity. This contrast would be lost if Paul were saying, "The spiritual gifts only last until the completion of Scripture—or until the rapture, or until the second coming, or until the maturing of the church." Paul is trying to contrast what is temporal with what is eternal. If "that which is perfect" is identified as

71

anything short of eternity, the contrast is severely weakened.

(d) This is the only view that explains the phrase "face to face" in verse 12. The only time we will ever see the manifestation of the *Shekinah* of God is when we enter into the eternal state. After the creation of a new heaven and a new earth, John saw the new Jerusalem descend from God to the earth (Rev. 21:1-2). Then in Revelation 21:11 and 23 he speaks of the glory of God being present there, lighting the city. In this place of our eternal abode, we will see His glory face to face (cf. Rev. 22:4).

You may ask, "What about the kingdom? Won't all believers see His glory in the kingdom?" No. In the kingdom there will be believing people living on earth who are still in their physical bodies while the New Jerusalem (where the glorified saints of the church age will be living) is suspended over the earth. God will dwell in the New Jerusalem, so the people on earth will not see His glory. They will, however, see His Son manifest on the earth. The fulfillment of "face to face" doesn't occur historically until the kingdom ends and God's glory is manifest to all the saints.

(e) This is the only view that explains the statement "then shall I know even as I am known" in verse 12. The only time we'll know as much as there is to know is when we're in heaven. Then we will have perfect knowledge because we'll be like Christ.

Historically, the perfect thing of verse 10 is the eternal state. But personally, we enter the eternal state whenever we go to be with Jesus Christ. If I died right now, I would immediately enter into the presence of God. Paul said, "We are confident, I say, and willing rather to be absent from the body, and to be present with the Lord" (2 Cor. 5:8). John told us that when Christ returns "we shall be like him; for we shall see him as he is" (1 John 3:2b). That's the eternal state for us. If we live until the rapture, that's when the eternal state begins for us. Historically, then, the eternal state begins after the millennial kingdom in the new heaven and the new earth when all the saints of all the ages are glorified and made perfect. The personal aspect of the eternal state is the perfection that comes the moment we go to be with Christ. The minute we enter His presence there is no longer any need for teaching, preaching, Bible study, classes, or any of those things. Why? Because we will have instant knowledge and insight. This is the only view that fits the context.

Paul's argument in 1 Corinthians 13 is to contrast love and spiritual gifts. In verse 8 he says that gifts are temporary but love is eternal. In verses 9, 10, and 12 he says that the gifts are partial but love is complete.

C. Gifts Are Elementary—Love Is Mature (v. 11)

"When I was a child, I spoke as a child, I understood as a child, I thought as a child; but when I became a man, I put away childish things."

I believe verse 11 is a personal word from Paul to illustrate his argument. For a Jewish boy, maturity wasn't a process; it resulted when he had his bar mitzvah. The day before his bar mitzvah he was immature; but once he had his bar mitzvah, he was mature, a son of the law. Paul was saying, "I'll deal with these elementary things until I have my spiritual bar mitzvah. But when that happens I'll be like Jesus, and I'll be able to put those childish things away. When I arrive at heaven, there won't be any more preaching or teaching for me to do. I'll be able to simply enjoy God without going through the work."

If gifts are limited to time, and love is forever, what should we put our emphasis on? Love.

IV. THE PREEMINENCE OF LOVE (v. 13)

"Now abideth faith, hope, love, these three; but the greatest of these is love."

Do you know why love is greater than faith and hope? Because faith is going to come to an end. Right now we walk by faith, not by sight (2 Cor. 5:7); but someday we'll walk by sight, not by faith. The same holds true for hope. Right now we have hope; but that hope will disappear once what we're hoping for is realized (Rom. 8:24-25). Both faith and hope are going to disappear, but love is eternal. That's why Paul says, "The greatest of these is love."

Your gifts, abilities, ministries, talents, faith, and hope—all of these are important. But they are temporal. Love, on the other hand, is forever. The point is this: you'd better learn to love, because it's the only link you can have with eternity. That's how important love is in the assembly of believing people. In fact, it's so important Paul's next three words are, "Follow after love" (1 Cor. 14:1a). That's the more excellent way!

Focusing on the Facts

1. Why is it significant that the gift of tongues is not mentioned in 1 Corinthians 13:9-13 (see p. 59)?
2. Why did Paul consider the gift of prophecy only a partial gift (see p. 60)?
3. What is the gift of knowledge? Why did Paul consider this gift a partial gift (see p. 60)?
4. Why do Bible teachers with a solid grasp of Scripture often disagree on certain points of doctrine (see pp. 60-61)?
5. Why is it beyond our capabilities to fully understand the nature of God (see p. 61)?
6. Does the fact that we have only a portion of the truth mean that the knowledge we have is wrong or unreliable? Explain (see p. 62).
7. Do we need more information than what God has given us? Explain (see p. 62).
8. What are two reasons God didn't give us all the truth there is to know (see pp. 62-63)?

9. What did Paul mean when he said, "For now we see in a mirror darkly" (1 Cor. 13:12a)? Why was this illustration appropriate for the Corinthians (see pp. 63-64)?

10. According to 1 Corinthians 13:10, when will we have full knowledge (see p. 64)?

11. What are the five views that attempt to identify "that which is perfect"(see pp. 64-73)?

12. The view that identifies the perfect thing as the completion of Scripture is weak for a number of reasons. What are these reasons (see pp. 65-67)?

13. What is probably the most common view of the identity of the perfect thing? What are the problems with this view (see pp. 67-68)?

14. What is the basis behind the view that the perfect thing is the maturing of the church? What are the weaknesses of this view (see p. 68)?

15. Based on the Greek text, why can't the perfect thing be the rapture or the second coming (see pp. 68-71)?

16. Will there be preaching or teaching in the millennial kingdom? How do we know? Why is this such an important point (see pp. 69-70)?

17. Of the five views given for the identity of the perfect thing, which one is the strongest? What are five reasons that support this view (see pp. 71-73)?

18. Explain the difference between the historical aspect and the personal aspect of the perfect thing (see pp. 72-73).

19. What is Paul's contrast in 1 Corinthians 13:11? What is the personal illustration behind this contrast (see p. 73)?

20. Why is love greater than faith and hope (see p. 74)?

Pondering the Principles

1. Do you understand how Jesus could be 100 percent God and 100 percent man? Do you understand why people are responsible to respond to the gospel if God has already sovereignly chosen them for salvation? Do you understand how one God can exist in three distinct Persons simultaneously? Do you know what happens to babies in the rapture? What about the unborn? Do you know when the rapture will occur? There are many things that God has not revealed to us. Our knowledge, therefore, is partial. Sometimes we try so hard to systematize and compartmentalize God that we lose sight of the fact that our under-

standing of God is limited. And when that happens we try to explain things that have no explanation. If you are someone who has to have an answer for everything, ask God to help you to accept the fact that His ways are higher than your ways. Also, ask Him to help you to be able to live with some of the obvious tensions or apparent paradoxes of Scripture. Then memorize and meditate on Romans 11:33.

2. Your spiritual gifts, abilities, ministries, talents, faith, and hope are all insignificant in comparison to love. Why? Because only love is eternal. Where are you concentrating your efforts? Are you committed to love? Read over the qualities of love in 1 Corinthians 13:4-7. In which of these qualities are you weakest? Step out in faith, and ask God to bring circumstances into your life that will strengthen the weak areas in your overall ability to love. And when those circumstances do come, remember that love is the greatest of all Christian virtues—the only one that is eternal.

4
The Truth About Tongues—Part 1

Outline

Introduction
A. The Corinthian Background of Tongues
    1. The infiltration of Corinth into the church
    2. The involvement of tongues in paganism
       a) The ecstasy of the Greco-Roman world
       b) The eroticism of the Greek world
B. The Charismatic Reproduction of Corinth
C. The Counterfeit Activity of Satan
D. The Chaotic Worship of the Corinthians

Lesson
  I. The Position of the Gift of Tongues: It Is Secondary (vv. 1-19)
    A. Prophecy Edifies the Entire Congregation (vv. 1-5)
       1. The pursuit of prophecy (v. 1)
          a) "Follow after love"
          b) "Desire spiritual gifts"
          c) "But rather [lit., "most of all"] that ye may prophesy"
       2. The perversion of tongues (v. 2)
          a) The principal purpose violated
          b) The private prayer language condemned
       3. The products of prophecy (v. 3)
       4. The prostitution of tongues (v. 4)
          a) The inability of tongues to edify the church
          b) The use of tongues to edify oneself
             (1) 1 Corinthians 8:10-11
             (2) 1 Corinthians 10:23-24
       5. The place of tongues (v. 5)
          a) The emphasis of hyperbole (v. 5*a*)
          b) The excellence of prophecy (v. 5*b*)

Introduction

At the Tower of Babel, God confused the languages of mankind. The only other biblical incident that can rival that confusion of languages is the confusion of tongues at Corinth. The church had so confused their understanding of the gift of tongues that they had substituted a satanic counterfeit for reality. Therefore Paul had to write an entire chapter to deal with that issue.

When we studied chapter 13 we saw that God did give a true gift of languages to the early church. It was only one of the miraculous sign gifts that God gave to the early church to authenticate the message of the new age. The writer of Hebrews tells us that "God, who at sundry times and in diverse manners spoke in time past unto the fathers by the prophets, hath in these last days spoken unto us by his Son" (1:1-2a). There was a new message, so to let the world know (particularly the Jewish world) that this was a new era and that God was speaking again, there were attendant signs and wonders. One of those signs was the ability that the apostles were given (and some who worked with them) to speak a language they did not know. That was the gift of languages, or tongues.

In previous lessons we learned that the gift of tongues was the ability to speak a foreign language. It was always a known language. For example, when the disciples spoke in tongues on the Day of Pentecost in Acts 2, verse 6 tells us that "every man heard them speak in his own language." But as we come to the Corinthian situation, we find that they had counterfeited the real gift of tongues and substituted an ecstatic kind of speech that was common in pagan religions.

A. The Corinthian Background of Tongues

  1. The infiltration of Corinth into the church

     The Corinthian church had allowed the entire world system in which they existed to infiltrate their assembly. For example, they were emphasizing human philosophies (chaps. 1-4), they were into hero worship (chap. 3), they were involved in terrible, gross, sexual immorality (chaps. 5-6), they were suing each other in court (chap. 6), they had misevaluated their home and marriage relationships (chap. 7), they were confused about pagan feasts, idolatry, and things offered to idols (chaps. 8-10), they had relinquished the proper place of women in the church (chap. 11), they had misunderstood the whole dimension of spiritual gifts (chap. 12), and they had lost hold of the greatest thing—love (chap. 13).

They allowed the satanic system that existed in their society to infiltrate the church. And with it came the pagan religious practices—with all the attendant ecstasy, eroticism, and sensuality. The Corinthians accepted it all, creating a confused amalgamation of truth and error.

2. The involvement of tongues in paganism

   a) The ecstasy of the Greco-Roman world

   At the time of the Corinthian church, the Greco-Roman world had a multitude of gods. In their worship of these gods, it was common for a person to go into ecstasy, which literally means "to go out of oneself." They would go into an unconscious state where all kinds of psychic phenomena would occur. They believed that when they were in an ecstatic trance, they actually left their bodies, ascended into space, connected up to whatever deity they were worshiping, and would begin to commune with that deity. Once they began to commune with that deity, they would begin to speak the language of the gods. This was a common practice in their culture. In fact, the term used in 1 Corinthians to refer to speaking in tongues (*glossais lalein*) was not invented by Bible writers. It was a term used commonly in the Greco-Roman culture to speak of the pagan language of the gods that occurred while the speaker was in an ecstatic trance. This language of the gods was always gibberish.

   b) The eroticism of the Greek world

   The Greeks had a word for this ecstatic religious experience. It was the word *erōs*. Sometimes translated as sensual love, the word *erōs* had a broader meaning. It meant "the desire for the sensual" or "the desire for the ultimate experience or feeling." Their religion, then, was an erotic, sensual, ecstatic religion —designed to be felt. In fact, when people went to their various temples to worship, they would actually enter into orgies with the temple priestesses. The erotic, sexual, sensual, ecstatic religion was combined with the gibberish of divine utterances. And these mystery religions, which had been spawned in Babylon, found their way into the Corinthian society—and the church.

B. The Charismatic Reproduction of Corinth

I'm afraid that what has happened today in the charismatic movement is a reproduction of exactly what happened in Corinth. Because of a deadness in the church, because of years of ignoring of the true work of the Holy Spirit, because of a lack of good Bible teaching, and because of dearth of anything really significant going on in the church, the people began to reach out to feel God and to sense His reality. That paved the way for Satan's counterfeit to come flooding in. As in Corinth, the charismatic movement has integrated pagan practices with Christianity. They have developed a sensual, feeling-oriented, experimental, erotic kind of approach to Christianity, and call it the work of the Holy Spirit. However, it is most likely the counterfeit of Satan.

An Emotional Experience

In his "Spirit Manifestations and the Gift of Tongues," Sir Robert Anderson quotes from a pamphlet written by a former leader of the Pentecostal movement in India: "Finally I went to the mission at 328 W. Sixty-third St., Chicago . . . asking only one question, 'Why do I not receive the baptism? What is the matter with me?'. The good friends prayed with me and said that nothing was wrong, I only needed to wait.

"Praise the Lord they were right. For the first time I knelt at the altar on Sunday afternoon, March 17, the power began to seize me and I laughed all through the following communion service. In the evening about 11 P.M., I knelt with a few of the friends praying for me (Elder S— placed his hands on my head for a short time, several times during the afternoon and evening). After some little waiting I began to laugh, or rather my body was used to laugh with increasing power until I was flat on my back laughing at the top of my voice. On rising I found that I was drunk on the new wine . . . acting just like a drunken man in many ways and full of joy. On kneeling to meet the Lord again, I was suddenly seized with an irresistible power of beseeching with groanings that could not be uttered, asking the Lord to have mercy on me a sinner, and telling Him that I wanted to go all the way with Him. The power of this praying was too great for me to endure, and suddenly my eyes opened to see Elder S—, who had been standing a few feet distant, fall as though he had been struck. I was relieved, and in a few seconds was straight up in the air shouting, 'Glory' at the top of my voice. Again kneeling, my eyes grew dark, and I was rolled over onto the floor, lying there for some time nearly unconscious. Then coming to and kneeling, I felt my jaws and mouth being worked by a strange force. In a few seconds, some baby gibberish was uttered, then a few words in Chinese that I understood, and then several sentences in a strange tongue. This turned into singing, and I did not again speak in tongues until Wednesday, three days later" (p. 35).

What was going on there? All kinds of experiences that are based on feelings and emotion—experiences that are apprehended by the senses rather than the mind. These kind of experiences were common to pagan religions—not Christianity. For example, Plato, who lived from 429-347 B.C., wrote in his dialogues to Phaedrus and Timaeus about pagan ecstasies of speech. This was not anything that belonged to Christianity. The true gift of languages in Christianity was used only when someone who spoke the language was present. It was a sign that God was there and that God's people were speaking God's truth. Never was it intended to be confused with paganism.

C. The Counterfeit Activity of Satan

Whenever God does something, Satan tries to counterfeit it. To cloud the true revelatory work of the Holy Spirit in the early church, Satan put up a smoke screen that consisted of phony revelations, phony visions, and phony tongues. That's why the apostle John said that when someone comes along and begins telling you they speak for God, you'd better "test the spirits whether they are of God" (1 John 4:1). It's easy to fall prey to the phony. And because the Corinthians had decided to marry the spirit of the age, they became victims.

Remember, Satan is called "the god of this age" (2 Cor. 4:4) and "the prince of the power of the air, the spirit that now worketh in the sons of disobedience" (Eph. 2:2*b*). Satan not only wants to be like God (Isa. 14:12-14), he appears "transformed into an angel of light" (2 Cor. 11:14). He wants to counterfeit reality and trick the church into accepting that which is phony.

In Corinth, the counterfeit practices of heathenism had engulfed the church. I'm afraid the same thing is happening today. Those kind of ecstatic, sensual, feeling-oriented experiences, however, are never associated in the New Testament with the true work of the Holy Spirit. In fact, in 1 Corinthians 14:32 Paul says, "The spirits of the prophets are subject to the prophets." In other words, no one is ever to give up his spirit or lose control of himself. At the end of chapter 14, Paul's final word on this subject was, "Let all things be done decently and in order." It's not the Holy Spirit's way to have a worship service where everyone jumps up with his own psalm, doctrine, tongue, revelation, and interpretation (1 Cor. 14:26). That's nothing more than the confession of paganism that had engulfed the church.

D. The Chaotic Worship of the Corinthians

The mystery religions of Babylon, which dominated the Corinthian culture during Paul's day, had developed all kinds of rites, rituals, vows, baptisms, animal sacrifices, feasts, fasts, ablutions for sin (such as immersion in a frozen river or crawling on bleeding knees for miles), ecstatic speeches, visions, and prophecies. And all of it had entered, to one degree or another, into the Corinthian church, causing absolute chaos. People were actually standing up cursing Jesus in tongues, and people were saying, "It must be the Holy Spirit." That's why Paul had to write and tell them that "no man speaking by the Spirit of God calleth Jesus accursed" (1 Cor. 12:3). Their worship was total confusion. "The wild frenzy of the Greek paganism became madness in the Corinthian church," says one writer. "And they, like the pagans, no doubt uttered their ecstatic speech with foaming lips and streaming hair."

As much as I wish it weren't true, I'm convinced that what we see in today's charismatic movement is the same kind of situation that occurred in the Corinthian church—an engulfing of the church in pagan practices. That which is counterfeit has been accepted as reality because it impacts the emotions of people who sat, for a long time, in churches where they never got anything that changed their lives.

Now we'll begin our study of 1 Corinthians 14. I'm going to divide the chapter into three parts: the position of the gift of tongues (vv. 1-19), the purpose of the gift of tongues (vv. 20-25), and the procedure of the gift of tongues (vv. 26-40).

Lesson

I. THE POSITION OF THE GIFT OF TONGUES: IT IS SECONDARY (vv. 1-19)

In the first nineteen verses of 1 Corinthians 14, Paul establishes that the position of the gift of tongues is secondary relative to the other gifts—specifically, the gift of prophecy. He gives three reasons to support this.

A. Prophecy Edifies the Entire Congregation (vv. 1-5)

The gift of tongues is secondary to the gift of prophecy because tongues cannot edify, but prophecy can. What is significant about that? The purpose of the church when it meets together is edification. At the end of 14:26 Paul says, "Let all things be done unto edifying." At the end of 14:12 Paul tells the Corinthians to "seek that ye may excel to the edifying of the church." In other words, the purpose of the church when it meets together is edification. Throughout chapter 14, this same concept is repeated over and over again. For example, verse 4 says, "He that prophesieth edifieth the church." Verse 5 says, "That the church may receive edifying." Verse 31 says, "All prophesy one by one, that all may learn, and all may be comforted." The point is this: the church is to come together for edification—to be built up. Paul was saying, "Look, tongues cannot edify—especially the counterfeit kind that you have. But prophecy edifies the whole congregation." That's the basic proposition of the first five verses.

1. The pursuit of prophecy (v. 1)

"Follow after love, and desire spiritual gifts, but rather that ye may prophesy."

a) "Follow after love"

This phrase is really the end of chapter 13. Paul was saying, "I've just told you about love—the greatest thing there is. That's what you ought to pursue." In 12:31, which is best translated as an indicative because of the context, Paul was actually saying to the Corinthians, "You're coveting the showy gifts, but I show you a more excellent way. You're busy chasing the ego-building, up-front, dramatic gifts, but I want to show you a better way—seek love." Then he gives them a great statement on love in chapter 13, which is almost parenthetical. In 14:1 he picks up where he left off in chapter 12 and essentially says, "If you're going to earnestly seek something, then earnestly seek love."

The phrase "follow after" is the Greek word *diōkō*, which means "to chase, to run after, to pursue." Oftentimes it is translated "to persecute." It is to be so vehement, so excited, and so energized that you literally persecute something and dog its steps. Paul in effect said, "If you're going to chase after something, let it be love."

b) "Desire spiritual gifts"

Literally the text says, "Continue desiring spirituals." Because of the context, the word *desire* should be translated as a continuous imperative. And the word translated "and" (Gk., *de*) would be better translated "but," as a contrast rather than a statement of equivalent ideas. In other words, Paul is saying, "You are pursuing the showy gifts instead of pursuing love. But don't stop pursuing spiritual gifts, because you should want the ministry of the Holy Spirit through the gifts of the Spirit. I'm not saying don't have anything to do with gifts. I'm just saying to pursue love and continue to seek the spiritual realm, the realm of the operation of the Holy Spirit, the true things that the Spirit of God is doing."

c) "But rather [lit., "most of all"] that ye may prophesy"

Tongues are secondary. Paul was saying, "When you come together to worship, instead of having the chaos, confusion, and gibberish of tongues, you should have the clarity of prophecy."

The Greek verb translated "to prophesy" (*prophēteuō*) comes from the words *pro*, which means "before," and *phēmi*, which means "to speak." Literally, then, the verb *prophēteuō* means "to speak before." To prophesy is to speak before others. That's what I do from the pulpit—prophesy. You may say, "I thought to prophesy meant to predict the future." No. The idea of predicting the future never came along until the Middle Ages, when the English word took on that meaning. That isn't its meaning in the Greek language. *Prophēteuō* simply means "to speak before others." In essence Paul said, "Instead of everyone shouting at the same time in ecstatic gibberish, someone ought to stand up before everyone else and proclaim the Word of God." Proclaiming the Word of God ought to replace the chaos and confusion of tongues.

There were times in the early church when the gift of prophecy was revelatory. And there were also times when the gift involved reiterating revelation that had already been given. But the point I want to make is that the church is to come together to hear the Word of God spoken—not to hear an ecstatic and emotional free-for-all. All things are to be done to edify. We are to gather to hear God speak to us through men who have been given the gift of preaching and teaching.

85

Paul was saying, "More than seeking tongues, you should seek that which is intelligible—prophecy."

The obvious reason for the inferiority of tongues is that no one could understand what was being said. The only time the gift of tongues was ever to be used was when there was someone present who could understand what was being said, or when there was a connection to be made to Pentecost (that the Holy Spirit is for all people—the Jews [Acts 2], the Samaritans [Acts 8], the Gentiles [Acts 10], and the disciples of John the Baptist [Acts 19]). The gift of tongues was a sign gift and was never intended for edification. In fact, tongues were useless to edify the church by themselves. Edification could come only when they were interpreted by someone with the gift of interpretation. Its purpose was as a sign to show that God was speaking and that the prophets and apostles of the New Testament were truly representatives of the voice of God.

2. The perversion of tongues (v. 2)

"For he that speaketh in an unknown tongue speaketh not unto men, but unto God [lit., "a god"]; for no man understandeth him; however, in the spirit he speaketh mysteries."

a) The principal purpose violated

Paul was saying, "You people with your pagan ecstasies are not doing what all spiritual gifts were given to do—minister (or speak) to men. Rather, you are all wrapped up in speaking pagan mysteries in ecstatic speech to some god. No one can even understand what you're saying!" Paul's not referring to the mysteries (Gk., *mustērion*) of God or the mysteries that he taught; he's referring to the mysteries of paganism.

Here is the basic, bottom-line truth: all spiritual gifts are given for the purpose of ministering (or speaking) to people. No spiritual gift was ever given for the purpose of ministering to God. All spiritual gifts are given to build up the Body of Christ by ministering to the members of the Body. God doesn't need us to minister a spiritual gift to Him, because He's not incomplete. Paul was saying, "You have fallen down on the basic use of spiritual gifts—their use among people to build up the Body. The tongues speaking that you are involved in, however, is not for people; it's for a pagan god."

The word *God* does not have an article in the Greek text (the anarthrous construction). And because of the context, I believe it's better translated "a god" rather than referring to the true God. In other words, they were involved in ecstatic communication with some pagan god and speaking in pagan mysteries. And they were violating the principal purpose of spiritual gifts—the fact that they were to be ministered to other people in the Body of Christ. God certainly didn't need them to talk to Him in some ecstatic gibberish!

b) The private prayer language condemned

It's amazing to me that the modern charismatic movement is simply repeating the same error in which the Corinthian church was involved. Charismatics teach that the essential use of tongues is as a private prayer language to God. That is exactly what Paul is condemning here in this passage. He was saying, "You've missed the point of the true gift of tongues. This gift was designed to speak to men, like all the other gifts. But you are involved in some kind of communion with a pagan god speaking in pagan mysteries, and no one knows what you're saying. God certainly doesn't want to be talked to like that!"

Is There Biblical Evidence for a Private Prayer Language?

It was never God's intention to be addressed in a language that is incomprehensible to the speaker. If you examine every prayer in the Bible and every passage in the Bible on prayer, you will not find anything, anywhere, anytime that even suggests that prayer should ever be unintelligible. In fact, Jesus said the exact opposite. In Matthew 6:7 He says, "When ye pray, use not vain [meaning-

87

less] repetitions, as the pagans do." The phrase translated "vain repetitions" is the Greek word *battalogeō*. The verb *logeō* means "to speak," and the prefix *batta* is not even a word. It is a figure of speech that in English we call an onomatopoeia—the naming of something by a vocal imitation of the sound it makes. For example, we say that a bee goes buzz, or a zipper goes zip, or a plane goes whish. Those aren't words; they're onomatopoetic figures of speech. *Batta* isn't a word, either. What Jesus is literally saying in Matthew 6:7 is, "When you pray, don't say batta, batta, batta—the sound of the stammering, stuttering gibberish that the pagans offer to their gods. The Father isn't interested in that kind of communication." We are to pray intelligibly and "with the understanding" (1 Cor. 14:15).

When Jesus went into the Garden to pray to the Father, He didn't talk in a heavenly language. When Deity communed with Deity, it was in a language that was clear. When Jesus stood by the grave of Lazarus, He prayed before He raised him from the dead. John heard every word of that prayer and wrote it down exactly as He said it—clear and intelligible. John 17 is the intimate prayer between Jesus and the Father. It's all clear—translated beautifully into English from the original language. The point is this: there is no biblical evidence whatsoever of a private prayer language. We are to pray in an intelligible, understandable way.

The carnal Corinthians, with their desire for the showy, attention-getting, ego-building, emotionalistic gift of tongues, were using it as a badge of spirituality and saying, "I have reached such a spiritual plateau that I can now talk to the eternal God in my own private language." That is pure paganism. Paul wrote to them and said, "You have missed the whole point of the use of the true gift of tongues. You're supposed to speak to men with the true gift, but you're speaking to a god in mysteries." By the way, it was believed that these "mysteries" were hidden secrets that only the initiated could know. It was also believed that these mysteries were received from the god that they connected up with when they went into an ecstatic trance. They had really missed the point of the true gift of tongues.

3. The products of prophecy (v. 3)

"But he that prophesieth speaketh unto men to edification, and exhortation, and comfort."

Paul said, "When you come together, don't speak in an unknown tongue that no one understands. Rather, seek to prophesy." Then he lists three things that will happen when the Word of God is spoken: people will be built up, people will be encouraged to a new kind of behavior, and people will be comforted in their agonies and their hurts. Instead of coming together and saying, "Batta, batta, batta," they were to hear the proclamation of the Word of God.

4. The prostitution of tongues (v. 4)

"He that speaketh in an unknown tongue edifieth himself, but he that prophesieth edifieth the church."

Which is better? To edify oneself or to edify the church? What's the point of the whole chapter? The point of 1 Corinthians 14 is the edification of the church, not edifying oneself. We were not given spiritual gifts for ourselves. If a person takes a spiritual gift, however, and uses it just to edify himself, he has prostituted the gift. It's only to be used to build up the Body of Christ.

a) The inability of tongues to edify the church

You may say, "It says in verse 4 that you can speak in an unknown tongue and edify yourself." But Paul isn't saying that's something positive. His point is that it doesn't edify the church. You may ask, "But if the tongues are translated, they edify the church, don't they?" Yes, but it was the gift of interpretation that edified, not the gift of tongues. The gift of tongues was useless by itself to edify the church, because no one knew what was being said. It would always have to be translated first. That's what he says at the end of verse 5: "Except he interpret, that the church may receive edifying."

It's wonderful to know that when the true gift of tongues was used as a sign and other Christians were present, God would always have someone there with the gift of interpretation to interpret what was being said. Why? So that it would not go without meaning to the church. God gave the gift of interpretation so that the church would be edified. God never wanted anything going on in the church that didn't build up. The Corinthians, however, were using the gift in a chaotic way. Not only that, they had determined that it would edify the church all by itself. But it won't.

b) The use of tongues to edify oneself

The Corinthians abused the gift of tongues in two ways. First, they had perverted the fact that spiritual gifts are meant for people, not God. Second, they had perverted the fact that spiritual gifts are meant for others, not oneself. This same perversion is still going on today.

Donald Gee, a well-known charismatic, wrote the following statement: "The revealed purposes of the gift of tongues are chiefly devotional, and we do well to emphasize the fact" (*Concerning Spiritual Gifts* [Springfield: Gospel Publishing House, 1937], p. 59). Another charismatic, Larry Christenson, wrote, "One speaks in tongues, for the most part, in his private devotions. This is by far its most important use and value" (*Speaking in Tongues and Its Significance for the Church* [Minneapolis: Bethany Fellowship, 1968], p. 28). That is the opposite of what Paul is saying in 1 Corinthians. He is saying, "Your gift is not to speak to God, and it's not for you. Your gift is for others in the Body. If you seek to edify God, or yourself, you're out of line."

When Paul said, "He that speaketh in an unknown tongue edifieth himself," it's possible that he was being sarcastic. So far in this epistle, Paul has already dealt with the whole idea of self-edification in a rather pointed way.

(1) 1 Corinthians 8:10-11—In this chapter Paul is telling the Corinthians, "It's not wrong to eat meat offered to idols. But because there are some weak Christians who believe it's wrong, don't do it—or you'll make them stumble." In verses 10-11 he says, "If any man see thee, who hast knowledge [i.e., you're a mature Christian], sitting at the table in the idol's temple, shall not the conscience of him who is weak be emboldened [Gk., *oikodomeō*, "built up, edified"] to eat those things which are offered to idols, and through thy knowledge shall the weak brother perish?" In other words, it is possible to edify someone to his harm. In this case, edification would cause a weaker brother ruin.

Edification can be for good or for bad. In chapter 14, the point is that if you use a gift to build up the church, it's for good. If you use the gift just to build yourself up, it's an act of selfishness. The word *edify*, then, can be for good or for bad; you have to find some qualifying principles.

(2) 1 Corinthians 10:23-24—Paul said, "All things are lawful for me, but all things are not expedient; all things are lawful for me, but all things edify not." Edify whom? Look at verse 24, "Let no man seek his own [edification], but every man another's [edification]." Do you see the point? Paul was saying, "All things might be OK for you, but don't do them because they're OK for you—do them because they're going to mean something to someone else." That's the point of all spiritual gifts. They're not for God and they're not for you; they're for the church. Paul said, "When you come together, instead of everyone seeking his own edification, seek to love one another." Why? Because love "seeketh not its own" (1 Cor. 13:5).

Paul is saying in 1 Corinthians 14, "Tongues can't edify the church. Furthermore, if you have the true gift of tongues and you use for self-edification, you're misusing the gift. Use it for what God intended. Otherwise, even if you were able to speak with the tongues of men and of angels, if you are seeking your own edification, you don't have love. And without love, you're nothing more than sounding brass and a tinkling cymbal."

5. The place of tongues (v. 5)

Finally in this section, Paul balances his strong words on the secondary nature and the uselessness of tongues to edify by acknowledging that there is a true gift of tongues and that it does have a true place.

a) The emphasis of hyperbole (v. 5*a*)

"I would that ye all spoke with tongues."

Why did Paul say that? The charismatics interpret it to say that Paul wanted everyone to speak in tongues. However, we have to take this statement of Paul's in light of other passages in 1 Corinthians. For example, in 12:30 Paul says, "Have all the gifts of healing? Do all speak with tongues? Do all interpret?" The implied answer is obviously no. And in 12:11 he says, "All these [gifts] worketh that one and the very same Spirit, dividing to every man severally as he will." Why does Paul say, "I wish you all spoke in tongues," if he knows they can't? I believe that he is speaking in hyperbole.

In 1 Corinthians 7:1-6 Paul talks about marriage as a good thing. Then in verse 7 he says, "I would that all men were even as I myself." In other words, "I wish you were all single." Now is that an actual divine mandate? No. That's wishing the impossible for the sake of emphasis—which is exactly what Paul is doing in 1 Corinthians 14. He's saying, "I'm not downplaying the gift of tongues. I wish everyone could have the real gift. But we know, of course, that that isn't possible." Paul was using hyperbole as an emphasis. He's balancing his strong words denying the primacy of tongues to emphasize the fact that there is a true gift.

b) The excellence of prophecy (v. 5b)

"But rather that ye prophesied; for greater is he that prophesieth than he that speaketh with tongues, except he interpret, that the church may receive edifying."

Paul said, "If I had my way it would be fine if everyone spoke in tongues; but if everyone was a proclaimer with the gift of prophecy, that would be even better!" But that isn't going to happen, either. Why does Paul say that prophesying is greater than speaking in tongues? Because unless tongues are interpreted, they don't do any good for the church.

In fact, those people who believe they have a great thing going with a private prayer language are severely mistaken. A private prayer language won't do anyone any good for the same reason that it won't do the church any good—there's no knowledge of what's being said. Consequently there's no learning in the mind, and it's nothing more than sensual ecstasy, a feeling, an emotion. Christianity has never been predicated on a feeling.

What does all this say to us in our day? Basically, two things. First, when the church comes together it is to hear the Word of God. Second, we need to keep pagan religious forms from infiltrating the truth of God's pure church.

There's an interesting footnote here. In verses 2 and 4 where it says "tongue," the King James translators put the word *unknown* preceding it. However, notice that in verse 5 where it says "tongues," the word *unknown* isn't there. Do you know why? It seems that the translators put the word *unknown* in with the singular word *tongue* and left it out with the plural word *tongues*. It's possible that they did this because they believed that Paul was using the singular to refer to the ecstatic gibberish and the plural to refer to the true gift (which would have been responsible for many languages [cf. Acts 2:6]). In verses 1-4 he is saying, "Your false gift is all wrong." But in verse 5 he is saying, "The true gift is all right when it's used properly and interpreted."

Let's be sure that when we come together, we come to hear the Word. Also, be constantly on guard against the infiltration of paganism into the church, because Satan hasn't changed his tactics. And remember, it's dangerous to seek something that God is not giving, because then you're wide open to Satan's counterfeit.

Focusing on the Facts

1. What were some of the effects of the satanic system of Corinth on the church at Corinth (see pp. 78-79)?
2. Describe the pagan worship of the Greco-Roman world of Paul's day and the role that speaking in tongues played in their worship (see p. 79).
3. What word did the Greeks use to refer to their ecstatic religious experiences (see p. 79)?
4. Why have many people in the church been drawn to the kind of feeling-oriented, experimental approach to Christianity that is characteristic of the charismatic movement (see p. 80)?
5. Why would Satan want to counterfeit the work of the Holy Spirit? Is he capable of accomplishing that? How can we guard against it (see pp. 80-82)?
6. How do we know that the chaotic worship of the pagans had entered into the Corinthian church (see pp. 82-83)?
7. In the first nineteen verses of 1 Corinthians 14, Paul establishes that the position of tongues is _____ _____ to that of the other gifts (see p. 83).
8. What is the purpose of the church when it meets together? Does the gift of tongues contribute to this purpose? Explain (see pp. 83-84).
9. According to 1 Corinthians 14:1, what does Paul tell the Corinthians to earnestly pursue? What had they been pursuing? What change did Paul want them to make in their perspective of what they were to consider important (see p. 84)?
10. When the Corinthians came together to worship, what spiritual gift was to have priority? Why (see p. 85)?

11. The literal meaning of the Greek word that is translated "to prophesy" is "_____ _____ _____" (see p. 85).

12. Why were tongues useless to edify the church by themselves (see p. 86)?

13. Is 1 Corinthians 14:2 a commendation of the Corinthians' practice of speaking in tongues, or is it a condemnation? Explain (see pp. 86-87).

14. What primary principle of spiritual gifts was being violated by the Corinthians in their use of tongues (see p. 86)?

15. Why is the word *God* in 1 Corinthians 14:2 better translated "a god" (see p. 87)?

16. What is the biblical evidence either for or against the use of a private prayer language (see pp. 87-88)?

17. What three things happen when the gift of prophecy is exercised (see p. 89)?

18. Why was it a prostitution of the gift of tongues to use it to edify oneself (see p. 89)?

19. Why did God give the temporary gift of interpretation to the early church (see pp. 89-90)?

20. According to charismatic Christians, what is the primary use of the gift of tongues today? How does this conflict with the proper use of any spiritual gift (see pp. 90-91)?

21. Is it possible to edify someone to his harm? Explain (see p. 91).

22. In light of 1 Corinthians 12:11 and 30, what is Paul saying in the first part of 14:5 (see p. 92)?

23. If the Corinthians had the ability to choose their spiritual gifts (which they didn't), what gift would Paul have wanted them to choose? Why (see p. 93)?

24. In 1 Corinthians 14, the King James translators inserted the word *unknown* in front of the singular word *tongue* and not in front of the plural word *tongues*. Why might they have done this (see pp. 93-94)?

Pondering the Principles

1. What are some of the philosophies and practices of the world that are infiltrating the church today? Why is this happening? What can be done to prevent it? What will you do to maintain the purity of the church?

2. How do you know whether something is of the Spirit or a counterfeit of Satan? What is the danger of making experience the basis of what is true (see John 17:17; 2 Cor. 11:13-15; 2 Tim. 3:13-17; 1 John 4:1)? What is the best way to guard against being seduced by that which is counterfeit?

5
The Truth About Tongues—Part 2

Outline

Introduction
A. A Charismatic Confrontation: The Motive
B. The Corinthians' Carnality: Its Manifestation
   1. The gift of tongues clarified
   2. The gift of tongues corrupted
   3. The gift of tongues corrected

Review
I. The Position of the Gift of Tongues: It Is Secondary (vv. 1-19)
   A. Prophecy Edifies the Entire Congregation (vv. 1-5)
      1. The pursuit of prophecy (v. 1)
      2. The perversion of tongues (v. 2)
      3. The products of prophecy (v. 3)
      4. The prostitution of tongues (v. 4)
      5. The place of tongues (v. 5)

Lesson
   B. Tongues Are Unintelligible (vv. 6-12)
      1. Identifying the problem (v. 6)
      2. Illustrating the principle (vv. 7-11)
         a) The use of sound (vv. 7-8)
            (1) Creating music (v. 7)
            (2) Calling to action (v. 8)
         b) The use of language (vv. 9-11)
            (1) It must be easy to understand (v. 9)
            (2) It must have meaning (vv. 10-11)
      3. Insisting on the priority (v. 12)

C. Tongues Produce an Emotional Effect (vv. 13-19)
1. The rejection of praying in tongues (vv. 13-14)
    a) Praying for an interpretation (v. 13)
       (1) The meaning
       (2) The misunderstanding
    b) Praying mindlessly (v. 14)
2. The requirement of one's understanding (v. 15)
    a) Praying with understanding (v. 15*a*)
    b) Singing with understanding (v. 15*b*)
3. The restriction of tongues (vv. 16-17)
    a) The inability to say amen (v. 16)
    b) The inability to edify others (v. 17)
4. The reaffirmation of tongues (v. 18)
5. The ranking of tongues (v. 19)

Conclusion
A. The Charismatic Repetition of the Problems
B. The Christian Response to the Principles

Introduction

A. A Charismatic Confrontation: The Motive

Let me begin by saying that I do not approach this text with an ulterior motive. My only motive is to understand what Paul is saying. I am not attempting to direct these messages on 1 Corinthians 14 to speak against the current charismatic movement. I'm simply trying to teach what the text is saying and then to make application. I know it's difficult for some people to accept the fact that I'm not personally attacking individuals who believe as the charismatics believe. However, I am endeavoring only to give a clear understanding of the things that are in the Word of God regarding the phenomenon of speaking in tongues, and how it applies to us today.

B. The Corinthians' Carnality: Its Manifestation

First Corinthians 14 brings us to the issue of tongues in the Corinthian Church—another manifestation of their carnality.

1. The gift of tongues clarified

The true, biblical presentation of the gift of languages (or tongues) can be seen in Acts 2:6 when the disciples spoke in tongues and the people heard them speaking in their own languages. The true gift of tongues is the miraculous ability to proclaim the truth of God in a foreign language unknown to the speaker. It also acted as a sign that God was present, by virtue of its miraculous element, and it authenticated the message that was being proclaimed.

There is no reason to believe that the clear definition and purpose for the gift of languages ever changed. The Greek terms used in 1 Corinthians 14 are the same words used in Acts 2. There is no new definition given. In other words, the gift of tongues in Acts 2 is the same gift that is mentioned by Paul in 1 Corinthians 14. It was still a miraculous ability to speak a foreign language that was unknown to the speaker, authenticating the message to someone who did know that language.

2. The gift of tongues corrupted

The confusion about tongues came because the Corinthians had corrupted this simple and clear gift by misusing it and by mixing it with the heathen concept of speaking in ecstatic gibberish common to their culture. It was relatively easy for Satan to counterfeit the true gift of tongues because of the pagan ecstasy that was so common to the Corinthian culture. But the true gift was uniquely of God—actual languages that could be understood. In the Corinthian assembly, they had counterfeited the real gift of tongues and had turned it into the ecstatic speech of the pagans. With its concomitant emotional excesses, it had begun to dominate the Corinthian assembly. Paul wrote 1 Corinthians 14 to separate the worship of false gods and the personal objective of self-satisfaction from the worship of the true God and the divine objective of reaching out to others. Paul wanted the Corinthians to use whatever gift they had (if it was really a true gift) to minister to others—not to use it selfishly to minister some special, ecstatic blessing to themselves.

Alexander Hay sums it up with the following statement: "These believers, in their heathen days, had believed that when they spoke in a tongue not understood by men, not even by the worshiper, they were speaking secrets or mysteries with their god. They believed it was their spirit speaking. The benefit was received by the worshiper alone; no one else understood. The worshiper profited through the ecstasy of feeling aroused and the sense that he was really participating with the spirits in the inner circle. He had no thought for the building up of the other worshipers. Paul contrasts this selfish objective with the Christian objective. The purpose of the manifestations of God's Spirit is that the whole congregation be edified" ("Counterfeit Speaking in Tongues," *What Is Wrong in the Church?* vol. 2 [Audubon, N.J.: New Testament Missionary Union, n.d.], p. 32).

Are There Two Kinds of Tongues?

Charismatics and Pentecostals realize that there is a difference between the tongues of Acts 2 and what is going on in 1 Corinthians 14. But they explain the difference by saying that there are two kinds of tongues. They say the tongues of Acts 2 are real languages and the tongues of 1 Corinthians 14 refer to an ecstatic, private devotional speech that one speaks in an unknown tongue to God personally and privately for self-edification. They recognize a difference and resolve the difference by saying there are two gifts of tongues.

I also recognize a difference, but I resolve it by seeing the true use of it in Acts 2 and the false use of it in 1 Corinthians 14. First Corinthians 14 doesn't talk about another gift; it talks about a perversion of the intended gift and its mixture with the heathen counterfeit. The Bible doesn't teach that there are two kinds of tongues speaking—one a language and one an ecstatic experience. In fact, the same term describes the gift in Acts 2 and in 1 Corinthians 14. So if God wanted to make a distinction, He would have used another term—but He didn't. It is the same word. It is the normal Greek word for language. There is no reason to justify the selfish use of tongues in 1 Corinthians 14 as if it were some new, special gift.

To say that what the Corinthians had was the true gift of tongues, being truly exercised, is to argue against the most basic truth of spirituality. The Corinthian church could never have been manifesting a true gift in the spiritual state they were in. They were worldly, divisive, opinionated, cliquish, carnal, fleshly, envious, strife-ridden, argumentative, puffed up, self-glorying, smug, immoral, compromising with sin, defrauding each other, fornicating, depriving in marriage, offending weaker Christians, lusting after evil things, idolatrous, fellowshiping with demons, insubordinate, gluttonous, drunken, selfish toward the poor, and desecrating the Lord's Table. How could they be expressing a true gift of the Holy Spirit? The answer is obvious. It would defy every single principle of spirituality if that were true. A believer either walks in the flesh or he walks in the Spirit. There is no argument about what the Corinthians were doing. They were walking in the flesh. And when you are walking in the flesh you are not manifesting a true gift in the true power of the Holy Spirit.

3. The gift of tongues corrected

As you come to 1 Corinthians 14, you must not conclude that the Corinthians were exercising the true gift of tongues. The only possible thing that could have been happening here was a misuse of the true gift. Why? Because everything else was wrong in their lives. Paul wrote the first thirteen chapters of 1 Corinthians to correct the errors in their assembly, and it's no different here. He wrote chapter 14 because their selfish, pagan use of ecstatic speech was being justified as the gift of languages given by the Holy Spirit. Apparently, even those who had the true gift had perverted it and were using it to speak in their own private way, as well as in the assembly when unbelievers weren't even present. They used the gift of tongues as a way to lift themselves up to a level of spiritual superiority. The Corinthian church had let every system in the world engulf them. Why would it be any different with the world's approach to religion?

Review

I. THE POSITION OF THE GIFT OF TONGUES: IT IS SECOND-ARY (vv. 1-19)

A. Prophecy Edifies the Entire Congregation (vv. 1-5; see pp. 83-94)

1. The pursuit of prophecy (v. 1; see pp. 84-86)

"Follow after love, and desire spiritual gifts, but rather that ye may prophesy."

Why are we to desire prophecy? Because prophesying edifies the whole congregation. In seeking the manifestation of the gifts of the Spirit in your assembly, you're to seek that which will edify the whole congregation—the best gift. I want to point out something that I didn't mention in our last lesson. In verse 1 Paul is not speaking about an individual Christian seeking an individual gift. He is talking about the assembly. He is saying, "When the assembly meets together, you should seek the manifestation of the gift of prophesying from whoever has that gift." This view is apparent from the context of the chapter.

From chapters 11-14 Paul deals with the meeting times of the Corinthian assembly. None of it has reference to a private time or a personal relationship with God. It all speaks of how they were to behave in the assembly. For example, chapter 11 speaks of how women were to behave in the assembly. Chapter 11 also speaks of how they were to take care of the Lord's Table and the love feast when they met together. Chapter 12 speaks of how they were to minister their gifts in the assembly. Chapter 13 speaks of how they were to manifest love to one another when they met together. And chapter 14 speaks of how they were to use the gift of languages when they met together. The whole context of chapters 11-14 is how to behave in the assembly of the church. When charismatic and Pentecostal people take chapter 14 and make the gift of tongues relate to a private devotional language, they are taking that totally out of the context in which it exists. Paul was saying, "When you come together, instead of wanting the ecstatic manifestations that you are involved in, seek that you may see someone prophesy, so that God may speak to you out of His Word."

2. The perversion of tongues (v. 2; see pp. 86-88)

"For he that speaketh in an unknown tongue [ecstatic speech] speaketh not unto men, but unto God [lit., "a god"]; for no man understandeth him; however, in the spirit he speaketh mysteries."

In the last lesson I mentioned an interesting possibility that occurs in chapter 14. I'm not going to be dogmatic on this, but the more I study it the more I believe it may be true. The possibility is this: whenever the singular term *tongue* appears, Paul may well be referring to the ecstatic gift. And when the plural term *tongues* appears, he's referring to the true gift. The reason I say that is only real languages can be plural—gibberish cannot. There aren't many different kinds of gibberish; there is only one kind! You can't say, "What kind of gibberish do you speak?" That may well be why the King James translators put in the word *unknown* whenever the word *tongue* is used in the singular. Perhaps they recognized this nuance in Paul's writing.

Maybe what Paul is saying here in verse 2 is, "He that speaks in this ecstatic gibberish, speaks not unto men, but unto a god. For nobody understands him, including the true God. That's not His kind of talk. However, in his spirit he is speaking mysteries." (Remember, the term *mystery* was the key word in all the pagan mystery religions.) In other words, "When you speak in your ecstasies, you are not speaking to anyone." Right there is the first perversion of the gift of tongues, because all gifts were intended to build up others rather than yourself.

3. The products of prophecy (v. 3; see p. 89)

> "But he that prophesieth speaketh unto men to edifica-
> tion, and exhortation, and comfort."

Paul contrasted their pagan, ecstatic speech with prophesying—which truly speaks the truth of God to the
hearts of people. That's a tremendous contrast. Then
Paul continues on and hits the issue of their selfishness
in verse 4.

4. The prostitution of tongues (v. 4; see pp. 89-92)

> "He that speaketh in an unknown tongue [gibberish]
> edifieth himself, but he that prophesieth edifieth the
> church."

I pointed out to you in the last lesson that the self-edification mentioned in this verse is not a good thing. In 1
Corinthians 8:10 we looked at an illustration of a bad
kind of edification—building someone up to a position
where he will fall. We also saw that in 1 Corinthians
10:23-24 Paul says, "All things are lawful for me, but all
things are not expedient; all things are lawful for me,
but all things edify not. Let no man seek his own [edifi-
cation], but every man another's [edification]." Since
self-edification and the wrong kind of edification are already in Paul's vocabulary as negatives, I believe it's
easy to see it here—he's pointing out their self-centered-
ness. He's saying, "He that speaks this gibberish is only
building himself up, but the one who prophesies truly
builds up the church. In the assembly there's no place
for this kind of ecstatic speech."

5. The place of tongues (v. 5; pp. 92-94)

> "I would that ye all spoke with tongues [the plural indi-
> cates the true gift of languages] but rather that ye proph-
> esied; for greater is he that prophesieth than he that
> speaketh with tongues [languages], except he interpret,
> that the church may receive edifying."

The true gift is all right if it's used in the right context: if someone who speaks that language is present, and if it's truly interpreted for the church to understand. But apart from that situation it has no purpose. Since prophesying edifies the whole church, the true gift of tongues takes a secondary place. The false gift has no place at all.

Lesson

B. Tongues Are Unintelligible (vv. 6-12)

1. Identifying the problem (v. 6)

"Now, brethren, if I come unto you speaking with tongues [languages], what shall I profit you, except I shall speak to you either by revelation, or by knowledge, or by prophesying, or by doctrine?"

In other words, Paul was saying, "Even if I, Paul the apostle, come to you and speak with the true gift of languages, what good will it do you? You speak Greek; you don't need me to speak another language to you. It wouldn't profit you."

It's amazing to me that anyone in the church would ever put such an incredible premium on unintelligible communication—communication that no one, not even the speaker, understands. It's also amazing to note that many times when the so-called interpretation is given, it can be proved that it is not a true interpretation at all. There are many testimonies to the effect that people have experimented by speaking Hebrew or other known foreign languages, and the interpretation given had nothing to do with what was actually said!

For some unknown reason, the modern charismatic movement has created a spiritual hierarchy where those who communicate in ecstatic gibberish no one understands are highly regarded. But the apostle Paul says, "If I came into your assembly and used the true gift of languages, it wouldn't mean anything to you because you speak Greek."

2. Illustrating the principle (vv. 7-11)

a) The use of sound (vv. 7-8)

(1) Creating music (v. 7)

"Even things without life, giving sound, whether flute or harp, except they give a distinction in the sounds, how shall it be known what is piped or harped?"

The flute and the harp were the most common instruments of that day. They were used at banquets, funerals, and religious ceremonies. The Corinthians would understand what Paul was referring to. The phrase "things without life" refers to these inanimate instruments that were known for beautiful music and the moods of joy and sorrow they could create. The phrase "except they give a distinction" means that unless these instruments are played with a distinction in tone and rhythm, their sounds mean absolutely nothing. The Greek text literally says "unless there is a difference." In other words, there has to be variation in sound to make sense. Paul was saying, "Sound alone, even from a beautiful instrument, means nothing unless there is enough variation in the tone for someone to discern a recognizable pattern or melody."

What's the point of that analogy? Only this: you can't be benefited or edified when you hear someone speak unless there is an understood variation in tone that communicates meaning. Paul was saying, "It doesn't do any good to do it any other way." Even the true gift of languages used with people who don't understand it is useless—to say nothing of gibberish, which is always useless.

(2) Calling to action (v. 8)

"For if the trumpet give an uncertain sound, who shall prepare himself to the battle?"

Can you imagine what would happen if the bugler who was supposed to trumpet the alert to prepare the troops for battle instead got up and blew any tune he wanted? The soldiers wouldn't know whether to get out of bed, go back to bed, put on their armor, or what. It's obvious that the trumpet cry has to have significant variation to have meaning. A military trumpet was the clearest and loudest of all instruments, but no soldiers would have any idea what to do if the bugle made an unintelligible sound.

b) The use of language (vv. 9-11)

(1) It must be easy to understand (v. 9)

"So likewise ye, except ye utter by the tongue words easy to be understood, how shall it be known what is spoken? For ye shall speak into the air."

Paul's point is that gibberish is worthless because no one is able to understand it. The only significant time for the use of the true gift in the apostolic era was when someone was present who understood the language. If it occurred in the assembly of believers, it would be translated in order that the believers might also be edified by it. But if it wasn't understandable, they were merely blowing into the air.

Paul was drawing some vivid pictures for the Corinthians—musical instruments so out of tune that they can't be recognized, and an army bugler so incompetent that the army has no idea what's going on. Then he said, "That's what's been going on in the Corinthian assembly—pure confusion and chaos." Paul was trying to help these believers to recognize and realize that the purpose of the gifts of the Spirit is to proclaim the gospel to the unsaved and to teach the truth to God's people—and in some cases, to authenticate those who would do both those things. And that can be done only through intelligible words. With irony, a touch of sarcasm, much patience, and great illustrations, Paul was trying to break through the barrier of ignorance, emotion, and superstition that existed in the Corinthian church.

(2) It must have meaning (vv. 10-11)

"There are, it may be, so many kinds of voices [lit., "sounds"] in the world, and none of them is without signification. Therefore, if I know not the meaning of the voice, I shall be unto him that speaketh a barbarian, and he that speaketh shall be a barbarian unto me."

Essentially Paul said, "If you don't talk in an understandable way, we're like two barbarians trying to talk to one another." Do you know what a barbarian is? To the Corinthians, a barbarian was a foreigner who didn't speak Greek. He was saying, "If you talk in that kind of stuff, we're going to be incommunicado. We would be like two barbarians without a common language."

The word *barbarian* (Gk., *barbaros*) is onomatopoeic. It is a word that sounds like what it refers to, like buzz, zip, and hiss. An onomatopoetic word simply repeats a sound. The word *barbaros* comes from the repetition of the sounds "bar, bar, bar." In other words, Paul is saying, "If you speak in unintelligible languages, I won't know the meaning of what you're saying. It will be nothing more than saying, 'Bar, bar, bar, bar' to me."

The whole point, then, is the uselessness of their unintelligible language of pagan gibberish. It had absolutely no significance whatsoever. And according to verse 10 it was contrary to all the laws of sound and meaning. Everything has meaning, except for what they were doing. All languages communicate, except for their kind. And remember, they could have been indicted for their misuse of the true gift by speaking a senseless language as if it were some great spiritual accomplishment and doing it when there was no one around who would even understand it.

No spiritual ministry can ever be accomplished with that kind of confusion. Unbelievers coming into their assembly would look around and say, "These people are mad!" (14:23). In other words, they would see that the frenzy of the Corinthians wasn't any different from the frenzy of the worshipers of Diana. They would see that the Corinthians were going through the same kind of ecstasy in which pagans were engaging. Consequently, they would see no difference between the Christian church and the temple of Diana.

3. Insisting on the priority (v. 12)

"Even so ye, forasmuch as ye are zealous of spiritual gifts, seek that ye may excel to the edifying of the church."

Paul essentially said, "Since you're so zealous of spiritual gifts, and you so want the manifestation of the Spirit, seek that which will truly edify the church. Incidentally, this is how Paul ends the first part of this chapter in verse 5 when he says to seek "that the church may receive edifying." In fact, this is the way he ends each of the various sections of this chapter because he's dealing with their selfishness. When the Corinthians came together, all of them were seeking this ecstatic, sensual experience. And we still have that today. Charismatics and Pentecostals are seeking a personal, ecstatic experience of speaking in tongues. But that is the antithesis of all spiritual gifts—gifts that are designed to edify the Body.

The position of tongues is secondary because, first of all, prophecy will edify the church. A second reason that tongues are secondary is that they are unintelligible and consequently have a limited use. Incidentally, that limited use was during the apostolic age only.

C. Tongues Produce an Emotional Effect (vv. 13-19)

1. The rejection of praying in tongues (vv. 13-14)

   a) Praying for an interpretation (v. 13)

   "Wherefore, let him that speaketh in an unknown tongue [gibberish] pray that he may interpret."

   This is a difficult verse to interpret. What did Paul mean when he said, "Let him that speaks in gibberish pray that he may interpret?"

   (1) The meaning

   As we know from our study already, the Corinthians were speaking in a private kind of ecstatic communication with a pagan god and thinking they were praying to the true God. But praying in gibberish was never the intention of the gift of tongues—it was a perversion. Paul was saying, "The one praying in gibberish ought to pray with the purpose of interpreting what he's praying." In other words, I believe Paul is being slightly sarcastic, saying, "You that are so busy praying in your gibberish, why don't you pray for something that will have meaning to someone?"

   In case you believe that's forcing the issue, read carefully through 1 Corinthians. You'll find that such sarcasm and irony is introduced on other occasions (e.g., 1 Cor. 4:7-14). In other words, "Let the one who is so anxious to pray in his private language pray instead for the gift that's intelligible. Let him ask God for something that the rest of the Body can benefit from because what he's doing is selfish."

(2) The misunderstanding

Someone may say, "You really pushed that inter-pretation into that verse." There's only one other way to interpret it. The other alternative is: "Wherefore, let him that speaks in an unknown tongue pray that he may receive the gift of inter-pretation." If we interpret it that way, the verse is saying we can seek certain gifts. It's saying that if we want the gift of interpretation, or any other gift, all we have to do is pray for it. Is that true? No. First Corinthians 12:11 says that the Holy Spirit gives the gifts to whomever He wills. And 1 Corinthians 12:30 says, "Do all speak with tongues? Do all interpret?" What is the answer implied by the sentence structure? No. God never said we can pray for any gift we want or that we can seek for any gift we want. Therefore, this verse can't be saying we ought to seek the gift of interpretation.

Another reason that verse 13 can't be interpreted as advocating a call to seek the gift of interpreta-tion is seen in verse 28. Paul said, "If there be no interpreter, let him keep silence in the church." In other words, if someone were going to use the true gift and speak in a language that an unsaved person in their midst would understand, he shouldn't use it unless he knows that there is an interpreter present who will interpret it for the church. Consequently, I also believe that they knew who among them had the gift of interpreta-tion. The true gift was so limited, then, that they couldn't even exercise it in the assembly if the person with the gift of interpretation wasn't there.

There is no way, then, that verse 13 can be exhorting an individual to seek the gift of interpretation. The only other alternative is that Paul is being slightly sar-castic here, saying, "While you're jabbering, why don't you pray something intelligent, like asking God for something that will benefit everyone else?"

b) Praying mindlessly (v. 14)

"For if I pray in an unknown tongue [gibberish], my spirit [Gk., *pneuma*, "breath, wind"] prayeth, but my understanding is unfruitful."

In other words, Paul was saying, "If I pray in gibberish, do you know what I'm doing? I'm just blowing a lot of hot air." The word *pneuma* can be translated "spirit," "breath," or "wind." Some would even say it refers to one's inner feelings. Charismatics, however, make the word *pneuma* refer to the Holy Spirit. However the text says "my spirit," not "the Holy Spirit." And even though it could be argued that the Holy Spirit is our spirit, it's compared in this verse with our understanding. So if the human understanding is on one end of the comparison, the human breath or spirit must be on the other end. They must be balanced.

Paul was saying, "If I'm praying in gibberish, my spirit may be praying, but it is unfruitful." In other words, there is nothing beneficial occurring. The gibberish of ecstatic tongues praying is mindless. "If I pray in an unknown tongue," Paul was saying, "I'm just blowing a lot of hot air, like the heathen. I won't understand what I'm saying, and neither will you." The counterfeit gift set up an emotional experience. It had no intellectual benefit at all.

You know as well as I do that there is never a time in the Word of God when God wants us to be mindless. There is never a time when God wants us to function on pure emotion without understanding. What was going on in Corinth, then, was wrong. They engaged in mindless, emotional experiences that had no meaning. In fact, in Matthew 22:37 Jesus says, "Thou shalt love the Lord, thy God, with all thy heart, and with all thy soul, and with all thy *mind*" (emphasis added). To pray or sing in a tongue is useless—useless to you and to anyone else. It is mindless emotion.

2. The requirement of one's understanding (v. 15)

a) Praying with understanding (v. 15a)

"What is it, then ["What is my conclusion?"]? I will pray with the spirit ["breath, wind, or inner being"], and I will pray with the understanding also."

Paul in effect said, "When I talk to God, it's going to come from inside of me. I'm going to use my breath (or my wind), but I'm also going to use my brain."

b) Singing with understanding (v. 15b)

"I will sing with the spirit ["breath, wind, inner being"], and I will sing with the understanding also."

Apparently the Corinthians used to sing in ecstatic languages as well as pray in them. Modern charismatics sing in tongues, too. But Paul said, "I don't do that. What purpose does that serve, except to show off to everyone that I have a private prayer language that hooks me up to God in a special way? I'm not going to do that. I'll pray with my breath and my mind, and I'll sing with my breath and my mind—not mindlessly."

When we pray in English, God understands. And when we sing in English, God understands. That's far superior than talking to God in some kind of gibberish—no matter what anyone tells you. God doesn't need that.

Should Musical Instruments Be Allowed in the Church?

The word *sing* in 1 Corinthians 14:15 originally meant "to play the harp." Through the years it came to mean "to sing to the accompaniment of the harp." There are some people who say that the church shouldn't have musical instruments, but that can't be supported biblically. In the New Testament and in the Septuagint, the word *sing* was understood to mean "to sing to the accompaniment of a harp." We can—and do—use musical instruments in the church.

3. The restriction of tongues (vv. 16-17)

   a) The inability to say amen (v. 16)

   "Else, when thou shalt bless with the spirit [without your mind], how shall he that occupieth the place of the unlearned say Amen at thy giving of thanks, seeing he understandeth not what thou sayest?"

   Notice the phrase "the place of the unlearned." In the Greek text the word is *idiōtēs*. Here it means "ignorant" and simply refers to someone whose ignorant of the language being spoken. In other words, if you speak in tongues, whoever is ignorant about the meaning of what you said can't even say "Amen" at the giving of your thanks. Why? Because he doesn't understand what you're saying.

   Amen is simply a Hebrew interjection that means "True, brother," "So let it be," or "I'm with you." And in the synagogue, saying amen was so important that you could hardly get your lesson done because of all the amens. Here are some quotes from the rabbis as preserved in the Talmud: "He who responds 'Amen' with all his might, has the gates of Paradise opened for him" (*Shabbath* 119*b*). "If a man says . . . a curtailed Amen, his days will be curtailed. But if one draws out the Amen, his days and years will be prolonged" (*Berakoth* 47*a*). Consequently, do you know what happened in a synagogue? It was a contest to see who could amen the most to get into the kingdom!

   This was also common in the early church—though much more genuine. Paul was saying, "If all you have is blind, emotional ecstasy going on, you can't agree on what to thank God for because no one knows what's happening." Do you get the point? When we come together, our spiritual gifts are for everyone's benefit. And if you're doing something that leaves someone out, it's wrong.

b) The inability to edify others (v. 17)

"For thou verily givest thanks well, but the other is not edified."

You might be doing a great job. And if you happen to have the true gift, in your own heart you might be thinking, "Boy, am I thankful to God." Unfortunately, no one else is edified, which makes the use of your gift wrong because you've missed the point of the assembly. You've missed the point of coming together.

Someone might say, "That's just why we teach that speaking in tongues is to be done in private." But that still misses the point of the gift, because it was never intended to be used in private. The gift of tongues was always to be used in the presence of someone who spoke the language. What good would it do to speak in tongues in private? In verse 17 Paul says that even if speaking in tongues is done in public, it doesn't do any good unless someone is there who understands what you're saying.

4. The reaffirmation of tongues (v. 18)

"I thank my God, I speak with tongues more than ye all."

Here Paul does the same thing that he did earlier in the chapter. Basically he says, "I've been kind of hard on the subject of tongues, and I don't want you to get the wrong idea. I do believe it's a true gift, and I thank God that I speak more languages than all of you." In a sense he's saying, "If you're wondering why I'm a little on the outside and don't quite understand all this ecstatic phenomena, I just want you to know that I've probably spoken in tongues more than any of you."

Paul had the true gift of tongues. Since he was an apostle, he had the gifts of an apostle (2 Cor. 12:12). He exercised those gifts, no doubt, as he traveled around. How did he use this gift? First of all, I'm sure he didn't use it as a private prayer language. Second, I'm sure he didn't use it in Christian meetings to show that he was spiritual. And third, I'm sure he didn't use it for his own benefit.

Let me tell you how he did use the gift of tongues. He used it when he traveled to a place where there were people who spoke a foreign language that he didn't know. In that kind of situation, he was given the ability by God to speak their language, so that they might know God was present and a miracle had happened. Then he would speak the truths of God, and they would be given the opportunity to be saved. Paul was a missionary to the Gentiles, so he might have had many instances in his missionary travels when he could have used this gift. It's interesting to me, however, that he ranked the gift of tongues so low. In fact, in all his writings he never refers to using this gift—except here in 1 Corinthians 14:18. And even here he doesn't give an illustration of when he used it.

5. The ranking of tongues (v. 19)

"Yet in the church I had rather speak five words with my understanding, that by my voice I might teach others also, than ten thousand words in an unknown tongue."

Paul in effect said, "The true gift of tongues is fine for evangelizing pagans in a language they understand and for showing them that God is present and that God is speaking. But in the church I'd rather speak five words that I understand, so that I might teach others, than ten thousand words in an unknown tongue."

Five words to ten thousand words is not actually the ratio. The Greek word translated "ten thousand" is *murioi*. And the reason this word is used here is that it was the largest number in Greek mathematics for which there was a word. For example, Revelation 5:11 speaks about the angels and says, "The number of them was ten thousand times ten thousand, and thousands of thousands." In the Greek text it keeps repeating the word *murioi* because it was the word that represented their biggest number. In the English, verse 19 would be more accurately translated, "I would rather say five words with my understanding than quintillion words in gibberish." In other words, there isn't even a comparison. Why? Because Paul wanted to teach people something they would understand.

Conclusion

A. The Charismatic Repetition of the Problems

Does this passage tell us how to govern tongues in the church? No, because the gift of tongues has ceased. Then what does this passage teach us? First, it shows us that the modern charismatic movement is simply repeating the same old Corinthian problem all over again. I say that with love and great concern—but I believe it's true. They use tongues in their assemblies today, they speak in gibberish, they do it for private self-edification, they seek the emotional experience rather than an intellectual understanding, they sing in tongues, they are absorbed in their own experiences, they glory in the unintelligible as if it were some secret communion with God, they do it among believers, and their missionaries do not have the true gift to reach people with different languages. What I see in the modern charismatic movement is a mirror of the Corinthian problem.

B. The Christian Response to the Principles

What are we to learn from this passage?

1. Exalt the proclamation and teaching of God's Word

2. Come together to hear and understand God's Word

3. Use spiritual gifts to build up one another

4. Never seek a selfish spiritual experience

5. Never seek an emotional experience; seek knowledge

6. Watch out for Satan's counterfeits

117

7. Do all things with a clear mind that is open to God's truth

8. Seek the true work of the Holy Spirit

Focusing on the Facts

1. What does Acts 2:6 tell us about the gift of tongues (see p. 99)?
2. When Paul mentions the true gift of tongues in 1 Corinthians 14, is this gift different from the gift of tongues in Acts 2 (see p. 99)?
3. Why was it relatively easy for Satan to counterfeit the true gift of tongues in the Corinthian church (see p. 99)?
4. What was the major reason Paul wrote 1 Corinthians 14 (see p. 99)?
5. What was wrong with the Corinthians' use of the gift of tongues (see pp. 99-100)?
6. How do charismatics explain the difference between the gift of tongues in Acts 2 and in 1 Corinthians 14? How is this difference more accurately resolved (see pp. 100-101)?
7. What is perhaps the strongest argument against the view that the Corinthians were exercising the true gift of tongues in the power of the Holy Spirit (see p. 101)?
8. In 1 Corinthians 14:1, how do we know that Paul isn't telling individual Christians to seek to have the gift of prophecy (see p. 102)?
9. How does the context of 1 Corinthians 11-14 relate to the issue of tongues as a private, devotional prayer language (see p. 102-3)?
10. What is the reasoning behind the possibility that when Paul mentions tongues in the plural, he's referring to the true gift, and when he mentions it in the singular, he's referring to ecstatic, pagan gibberish (see p. 103)?
11. Why wouldn't it profit the Corinthians for Paul to visit their church and speak in tongues (see p. 105)?
12. How does Paul illustrate the principle that tongues must be understood to be of any value (see pp. 106-7)?
13. Where does the Greek word for barbarian come from? Explain Paul's use of it in 1 Corinthians 14:11 (see p. 108).
14. If an unbeliever came into the Corinthian assembly during a worship service, what do you believe he would see and what conclusions would he reach (see p. 109)?

15. How was the Corinthians' use of the gift of tongues a violation of the use of any spiritual gift (see p. 109)?
16. What are three reasons that the gift of tongues is secondary to the gift of prophecy (see pp. 109-10)?
17. What are two ways that 1 Corinthians 14:13 could be interpreted? What's the most probable interpretation? Why (see pp. 110-11)?
18. Why doesn't the word *spirit* in 1 Corinthians 14:14 refer to the Holy Spirit? It refers to what (see p. 112)?
19. According to 1 Corinthians 14:14, why is praying in tongues a useless experience (see p. 112)?
20. How does the original meaning of the word *sing* in 1 Corinthians 14:15 support the use of musical instruments in the church (see p. 113)?
21. Who is it that occupies "the place of the unlearned" in 1 Corinthians 14:16? How were these people restricted in the Corinthian assembly (see p. 114)?
22. What does it mean to say amen? How did a Jew view the saying of amen during the teaching of a lesson in the synagogue (see p. 114)?
23. Why would it have been wrong if someone in the Corinthian assembly couldn't have said amen (see p. 114)?
24. If someone with the gift of interpretation wasn't present in the Corinthian assembly, why should even the true gift of tongues not be exercised (see p. 115)?
25. Was it proper for someone to speak in tongues if no one was present who spoke that particular foreign language? Explain (see p. 115).
26. Did Paul have the gift of tongues? Support your answer (see pp. 115-16).
27. Why would Paul have needed to use the gift of tongues in his ministry (see p. 116)?
28. Did Paul consider the gift of tongues an important gift to be exercised in the church? Explain (see pp. 116-17).
29. What should be our responses to the principles in 1 Corinthians 14:6-19 (see pp. 117-18)?

Pondering the Principles

1. What was the spiritual condition of the Corinthian church? Based on this spiritual condition, do you believe that they were exercising the true gifts of the Spirit in the power of the spirit?

Explain. What is your own spiritual condition right now? Are you walking in the Spirit or in the flesh (see Gal. 5:16-26)? Can you exercise a gift of the Spirit while walking in the flesh? If you attempt to do this, what does that gift become? What is the priority, then, before you can minister your spiritual gift in the power of the Spirit? Make a commitment to the Lord that you will take care of your relationship with Him before you attempt to minister your spiritual gift to others.

2. Look over "The Christian Response to the Principles" section on pages 117-18. In which of these principles are you already strong? In which are you weak? Go through each one of these principles, and either reaffirm your commitment to it or consider what steps you can take to become committed to it.

6
The Truth About Tongues—Part 3

Outline

Review
I. The Position of the Gift of Tongues: It Is Secondary (vv. 1-19)

Lesson
II. The Purpose of the Gift of Tongues: It Is a Sign (vv. 20-25)
   A. The Purpose Suggested
      1. Personal edification and devotion
         a) Described
         b) Disputed
      2. Evangelism
      3. Proof of Spirit baptism
         a) 1 Corinthians 12:13, 30
         b) Acts 2:38
         c) Acts 4:31
   B. The Purpose Stated (vv. 20-22)
      1. The problem of the Corinthians (v. 20)
         a) Their lack of understanding
         b) Their love of evil
      2. The purpose of tongues (vv. 21-22*a*)
         a) A sign of cursing
            (1) Old Testament warnings of judgment
               (*a*) Isaiah 28:7-12
               (*b*) Deuteronomy 28:49
               (*c*) Jeremiah 5:15
            (2) New Testament warnings of judgment
               (*a*) Proclaimed by Jesus
               (*b*) Presented in Acts
         b) A sign of blessing
         c) A sign of authority
      3. The priority of prophecy (v. 22*b*)

C. The Purpose Scrutinized (vv. 23-25)
1. The results of tongues in the assembly (v. 23)
2. The results of prophecy in the assembly (vv. 24-25)
   a) Conviction
   b) Judgment
   c) Exposure
   d) Worship

Review

In 1 Corinthians 14, the apostle Paul corrects the carnal Corinthians on the basis of their misuse and perversion of the gift of tongues (or languages). In the New Testament era, the true gift of tongues was the ability to speak a language that was unknown to the speaker but known to someone present. God had a definite purpose for this gift, which we'll see later on in this lesson, but the Corinthian assembly had taken the true gift and had twisted it for an untrue use. They also had added a counterfeit gift to the true gift.

It was common in the pagan mystery religions of that day for the people to believe they could enter into a state of frenzy or ecstasy, slip out of their bodies, and commune on another level with a deity. And when they supposedly did that, they would speak to that deity in an unknown language—the language of that god. They believed that this ecstatic, supernatural phenomenon was a great act of devotion toward that god. Consequently, it was self-edifying. As with other practices of the world's system, this pagan practice of speaking in ecstatic languages infiltrated the Corinthian church.

The Corinthian Christians actually believed that the gift of tongues was speaking an ecstatic babble or gibberish and communing with God in a private prayer language. The apostle Paul had to write this chapter to dispel that idea. He also wrote this chapter to make sure that when the true gift was exercised, it was exercised properly in the right context to accomplish the right purpose.

First Corinthians 14 is an urgent chapter for us today because it is often being said that speaking in tongues is necessary to realize the full manifestation of the Holy Spirit—the full expression of His power in our lives. Many are loudly crying out for all Christians to have this experience, so we need to understand exactly what Paul is saying here.

This chapter can be divided into basically three major points. In our last two lessons we talked about the position of the gift of tongues and saw that it was secondary. The second point, which we are going to look at in this lesson, is the purpose of the gift of tongues. And the third point, which we'll consider in the next lesson, is the procedure for the gift of tongues.

I. THE POSITION OF THE GIFT OF TONGUES: IT IS SECONDARY (vv. 1-19; see pp. 83-94, 102-18)

Lesson

II. THE PURPOSE OF THE GIFT OF TONGUES: IT IS A SIGN (vv. 20-25)

This is a vital area of study, because if we can determine the purpose of the gift of tongues then we will be able to evaluate what's going on today, or at any time in history, relative to this gift. It either fits the biblical purpose or it does not. Consequently, we can determine whether it's legitimate or not.

A. The Purpose Suggested

1. Personal edification and devotion

   a) Described

      Let me begin by reiterating what is often offered as the purpose of tongues—particularly today among our brothers and sisters in Pentecostal and charismatic fellowships. They tell us that the purpose of tongues is primarily for personal edification and devotion. In other words, they say it is to be used as a private prayer language because it builds a person up and allows him to have devotions with God in a supernatural way.

As we have already seen (p. 90), well-known writers in charismatic circles have emphasized that tongues are meant to edify oneself during a private devotional time. They see that as its primary usage. You read about little else.

So, it's being said that speaking in tongues is a new way to have your devotions, a new way to edify yourself, a new way to build yourself up, a new way for you to have communion with God and experience something deeper and more meaningful than you could experience any other way.

b) Disputed

In the first nineteen verses of 1 Corinthians 14, Paul basically chides the Corinthians for their selfish use of tongues. When we studied verse 2, I showed you that Paul was telling the Corinthians, "When you speak in ecstatic gibberish, you are doing what is done in the mystery religions by people who are speaking to their gods. This is not the design of any spiritual gift, because all spiritual gifts are designed to speak to men or to serve others." In 1 Corinthians 12:7 Paul says that the gifts were given to profit all. They had misused this gift.

All the gifts are to be used to edify one another. The idea of self-edification is a perversion. In 1 Corinthians 14:4 Paul says, "He that speaketh in an unknown tongue [lit., "gibberish"] edifieth himself." He is not telling them to speak in tongues to edify themselves; he's merely recognizing that this is what they are doing. What's wrong with edifying oneself? It's selfish; and no gift is ever to be used selfishly. Paul essentially said, "You are actually speaking in this gibberish for the purpose of building yourselves up. But the truth of the matter is that your understanding is unfruitful, and no one who hears you can even say amen. You are totally ignoring the people around you because you are selfish. As for me, I'd rather speak five words that others can understand than ten thousand words in a foreign language." They were speaking in tongues for self-edification, but that wasn't the point of the gift.

Tongues were never intended for the purpose of edification. In fact, tongues can't edify the church because the members don't understand what's being said. And when they are interpreted, it is the gift of interpretation that edifies—not the gift of tongues. Further, tongues can't edify an individual because his mind is disengaged and therefore unfruitful.

It isn't possible, then, that tongues can be defined biblically as a self-edifying prayer language to God. If you study prayer in the New Testament, you will never find a verse that tells you to pray to God in an unknown language. When Jesus laid out the model for prayer in Matthew 6:9-13, there wasn't any gibberish or ecstatic language involved. (In fact, in verse 7 He had just condemned such an approach to prayer.) People sometimes say, "But speaking in tongues is a method of praising God in a marvelous and free way." But if it's such a great way to praise God, and praise is the very character of heaven, why does 1 Corinthians 13:8 say that tongues will cease? We can't conclude that the gift of tongues is for self-edification or devotion.

2. Evangelism

Some people say that the gift of tongues in the New Testament was to enable someone to preach the gospel in another language. That sounds like a good idea. And I wouldn't deny that somewhere on a mission field, God may have given someone the ability to speak a language he didn't know to give the gospel to someone in a critical situation. However, it's not accurate to state that the purpose of the gift of tongues in the New Testament was to preach the gospel to people who didn't understand. Do you know why? Because there are no illustrations of the gift of tongues' being used like that in the New Testament.

You may ask, "What about in Acts 2 on the Day of Pentecost when the disciples spoke in tongues and everybody in the crowd heard them speak in his own language?" Do you know what the multitude heard? They heard them speaking "the wonderful works of God" (Acts 2:11). In other words, they went over the great historical events that God had done in the Old Testament. They were drawing the attention of the Jewish crowd so that Peter could stand up and preach the gospel to them in a language that was common to all (Acts 2:14-40). Rather than saying that the purpose of the gift of tongues was evangelism, you might say that it was more useful for pre-evangelism. It gathered the crowd, and then the gospel was preached in a commonly understood language.

Some have suggested that the gift of tongues is for edification, whereas others have suggested that it's for evangelism. But those don't really fit the New Testament pattern.

3. Proof of Spirit baptism

In studying 1 Corinthians 12, some people conclude that the gift of tongues is proof that the baptism of the Holy Spirit has taken place. There are several problems with this view, however, as seen in the following passages.

a) 1 Corinthians 12:13, 30—Paul wrote, "By one Spirit were we all baptized." How many were baptized? All. Look at verse 30: "Have all the gifts of healing? Do all speak with tongues? Do all interpret?" No. In other words, all are baptized, but all do not speak in tongues. You cannot equate those two. Verse 13 is telling us that the baptism of the Spirit is a nonexperiential reality that happens at the moment of salvation for all believers.

b) Acts 2:38—After Peter preached he said, "Repent, and be baptized, every one of you, in the name of Jesus Christ for [lit., "because of"] the remission of sins, and ye shall receive the gift of the Holy Spirit." Three thousand people responded to Peter's sermon

126

that day (v. 41). Scripture doesn't say that any of them spoke in tongues after they received the Holy Spirit.

c) Acts 4:31—Referring to the early church, Luke wrote, "When they had prayed, the place was shaken where they were assembled together; and they were all filled with the Holy Spirit." At that point, do you believe they all spoke in tongues? No. "They spoke the word of God with boldness."

In 1 Corinthians 12 all are baptized by the Spirit; in Acts 2 people receive the Spirit; and in Acts 4 people are filled with the Spirit. But in each of those cases an accompanying phenomenon of tongues is not mentioned. Therefore, you can't equate the baptism of the Spirit, the receiving of the Spirit, or the filling of the Spirit with speaking in tongues.

You may ask, "If speaking in tongues isn't a sign of Spirit baptism, and if it isn't for the purpose of actually proclaiming the gospel, and if it isn't for the purpose of building myself up in a private way, what is the gift of tongues for?"

B. The Purpose Stated (vv. 20-22)

1. The problem of the Corinthians (v. 20)

"Brethren, be not children [lit., "stop being children"] in understanding; however, in malice [Gk., *kakia*, "evil"] be ye children [lit., "infants"], but in understanding be men."

This is a strong indictment, so Paul begins by calling them "brethren" to conciliate them a little bit before he hammers them. The admonition suggests that because of their misuse of tongues they were practicing evil.

a) Their lack of understanding

Paul said that the Corinthians were "children in understanding." In other words, they hadn't grown up spiritually to the point where they understood solid

127

doctrine. They were "children, tossed to and fro, and carried about with every wind of doctrine" (Eph. 4:14). They didn't use their minds. In fact, 1 Corinthians 14:14 implies that their minds were unfruitful. They were not thinking through the right things—the biblical things—that they had received. Consequently, the Corinthians were "children in understanding" rather than mature people with minds that grasped the truth.

b) Their love of evil

The Corinthians should have been infants in malice and evil—but they weren't. What do I mean by that? Infants have no thoughts of evil or malice toward anyone. They're a symbol of love, gentleness, tenderness, and care. Paul was saying, "Why don't you be like that? Be little infants in regard to evil, yet mature in your thinking, instead of being infants in your thinking and mature in your evil."

Because of their selfish exercise of spiritual gifts for the purpose of self-edification, they were ignoring the rest of the family of God. There was no room for teaching the Word of God because of the total confusion that characterized their worship. In fact, not only couldn't the members of the church get anything out of the services, but also the people who visited their congregation believed they were insane because of the absolute chaos that occurred as everyone in the church did what was personally satisfying.

The problem in the Corinthian church boiled down to a preference of anti-intellectualism and existential experience—which is basically what we see happening today. A pervasive kind of anti-intellectualism has allowed the tongues movement to sweep into the church and accommodate that kind of thinking.

Paul said, "Stop being children, and start thinking like adults." After having said that and calling them to attention, Paul stated the purpose of tongues.

2. The purpose of tongues (vv. 21-22a)

> "In the law it is written, With men of other tongues and other lips will I speak unto this people; and yet for all that will they not hear me, saith the Lord. Wherefore, tongues are for a sign, not to them that believe, but to them that believe not."

If you never learn anything else about tongues, you can be sure about one thing: "Tongues are for a sign, not to them that believe, but to them that believe not." That statement alone is the heart of this chapter. In fact, if anyone today believes he has the gift of tongues, all he needs to do is to deal with the reality of that statement, and he will be forced to reconsider what he does. It couldn't be any simpler. Tongues are a sign to those who don't believe.

Basically, the purpose of tongues as a sign is threefold. They are a sign of cursing, a sign of blessing, and a sign of authority.

a) A sign of cursing

This is the primary purpose of the gift of tongues, according to these verses. Verse 21 says, "In the law [which can refer to the Pentateuch or the entire Old Testament] it is written [freely quoting Isaiah 28:11-12], With men of other tongues and other lips will I speak unto this people [referring to Israel]; and yet for all that will they not hear me, saith the Lord." Then, having stated that Old Testament proclamation of Isaiah to Israel, Paul applies it to the time of the Corinthians in verse 22, telling them that tongues have the same meaning in their own day: "Wherefore, tongues are for a sign, not to them that believe, but to them that believe not." Paul drew a conclusion from the Old Testament text. His conclusion was that tongues are not for believing people; they are for unbelieving people. What unbelieving people? The phrase "this people" in verse 21 is referring to

Israel, so tongues are specifically a sign to unbelieving Israel.

(1) Old Testament warnings of judgment

(a) Isaiah 28:7-12

In Isaiah 28 we find ourselves in the Southern Kingdom of Judah during the reign of King Hezekiah. The year is approximately 705 B.C. In 722 B.C., seventeen years earlier, the Northern Kingdom of Israel had been taken and destroyed by the Assyrians as a judgment of God on Israel's unbelief and apostasy. Now, in 705 B.C., the Southern Kingdom of Judah was also behaving in a terrible, disobedient manner. God spoke to them through the prophet Isaiah to warn them of their impending judgment. That is the message of the first fifteen verses of Isaiah 28. It was a warning from the prophet to the Southern Kingdom that they are going to receive the same kind of judgment that the kingdom in the north received.

In verse 7 Isaiah finds the leaders of Israel, the prophets, and the priests in a drunken stupor: "They also have erred through wine, and through strong drink are out of the way." They had failed to fulfill their function as leaders because they were drunk. Verse 7 continues, "The priest and the prophet have erred through strong drink; they are swallowed up of wine, they are out of the way through strong drink, they err in vision, they stumble in judgment."

Notice the ugliness of verse 8: "All tables are full of vomit and filthiness, so that there is no place clean." Isaiah found them at some party in a drunken stupor, having vomited all over the tables. So he delivered his message of rebuke and of coming judgment.

Do you know what their reaction was? They mocked him, scorned him, chided him, and derided him. They say in verse 9, "Whom shall he teach knowledge? And whom shall he make to understand doctrine? Those who are weaned from the milk, and drawn from the breasts." In other words, "Who could he ever teach? Only babies!" Why? "Because he always goes precept upon precept, line upon line, here a little and there a little. He must think we're babies. He keeps repeating the same simple stuff over and over again."

They mocked him. They didn't appreciate his attitude, so they began to sneer at the prophet and call his teaching simple and childish. He tried to teach them over and over again, but they never heard him. In verses 11-12 Isaiah says that God "with stammering lips and another tongue will . . . speak to this people. To whom he said, This is the rest by which ye may cause the weary to rest, and this is the refreshing; yet they would not hear." In other words God said, "You wouldn't hear the simple, repeated, childlike message of Isaiah, so I'm going to talk to you in a language you'll never understand." He was referring to the babbling Babylonians who had already encompassed their city, who would take them out of their land, destroy them, slaughter them, and burn them. And when they began to hear that unintelligible language of Babylonia, they would know that the judgment of God had fallen. By the way, the Babylonian invaders did come in 588 B.C. Because of Judah's unbelief and apostasy, God brought a terrible judgment.

(b) Deuteronomy 28:49

The people of Israel had been warned before the warning we saw in Isaiah. Back in the fifteenth century before Christ, Moses gives the following warning in Deuteronomy 28:49:

"The Lord shall bring a nation against thee from far, from the end of the earth, as swift as the eagle flieth; a nation whose tongue thou shalt not understand." I believe this warning could have reference to the destruction of Jerusalem in A.D. 70.

In the fifteenth century God warned them that when they heard a strange language, it would mean judgment. And in the eighth century, God warned them through the prophet Isaiah that when they heard a strange language it would mean judgment. There was also a similar warning in the sixth century by the prophet Jeremiah.

(c) Jeremiah 5:15

The great weeping prophet said, "Lo, I will bring a nation upon you from far, O house of Israel, saith the Lord; it is a mighty nation, it is an ancient nation, a nation whose language thou knowest not, neither understandest what they say."

In the Old Testament, then, God had clearly pointed out to the people of Israel that when they were going to be judged, there would be a sign. That sign was that they would hear a language they couldn't understand.

(2) New Testament warnings of judgment

When Paul quotes Isaiah 28 in 1 Corinthians 14, he is saying, "Look, just as when Moses, Isaiah, and Jeremiah said it, those languages are a sign to the unbeliever that God is about to act in judgment." But what did that mean in Paul's generation? When the Jewish people heard a multitude of languages they didn't understand on the Day of Pentecost, they should have known that the judgment of God was imminent. And it was! In A.D. 70 the Romans wiped out Jerusalem. And the sacrificial system of Judaism, which ceased when the Temple was destroyed, has never been restored. They should have known the judgment of God was going to fall.

If the judgment of God fell on the unbelief and apostasy of the Northern Kingdom in 722 B.C., and if the judgment of God fell on the unbelief and apostasy of the Southern Kingdom in 586 B.C., then it seems to me that God's judgment would certainly fall on a nation that turned its back on and crucified its own Messiah in the first century. And it did. It also seems to me that once the destruction of Jerusalem came in A.D. 70, the whole purpose for the gift of languages ceased. It did also. The gift of tongues was never intended to be something for a Christian. That's not my opinion; it's what 1 Corinthians 14:22 says. The gift of tongues was for a Jew who didn't believe, so that he might know God was going to act in judgment.

(a) Proclaimed by Jesus

In Luke 13:35 Jesus says, "Behold, your house is left unto you desolate." In Luke 21:20 He carries it a step further: "When ye shall see Jerusalem compassed with armies, then know that its desolation is near." Then in verse 24: "They shall fall by the edge of the sword, and shalt be led away captive into all nations; and Jerusalem shall be trodden down by the Gentiles." In other words, Jesus was saying, "Judgment is coming!"

(b) Presented in Acts

This purpose for the gift of tongues can be traced and verified in the book of Acts. In Acts 2, many unbelieving Jewish people are present. And later on in the book of Acts when speaking in tongues occurs (in chaps. 8, 10, and 19), even though there are no unbelieving Jews present, the message of judgment is still the same. The recurrence of the

133

same phenomenon that occurred at Pentecost reinforced in the minds of believing Jews that God was going to judge the nation of Israel. Also, when these believing Jews told their fellow countrymen what had occurred, God's judgment would again be confirmed.

First of all, and primarily, the gift of tongues is a sign of cursing to unbelieving Israel.

b) A sign of blessing

When tongues occurred at Pentecost, the message to Israel was: "God is not going to work exclusively through one nation any longer—speaking only one language. God's not going to favor one people any longer. Instead, He is going to go to the world and build His church." The very fact that all those languages were spoken at Pentecost was God's way of saying, "No more will I exclusively work through Israel. I'm going to speak in the world's languages and build the church"—a mystery hidden from the Old Testament writers (Eph. 3:2-6).

Primarily tongues are as a sign of the curse on Israel. But notice that a residual effect of that curse is the blessing that comes to the whole world. As Christ turned away from a rebellious people, He opened His arms to the world. The gift of tongues was also a sign of blessing, residually. Paul speaks to this issue in Romans 11:12 when he talks about the fall of the Jews becoming the riches of the world. Jerusalem was destroyed, and Israel was temporarily set aside —and the Gentiles became beneficiaries as God reached out to them.

At Pentecost, the disciples suddenly burst out declaring the wonderful works of God in every language (Acts 2:11). This was an unmistakable sign that a transition had come—a curse on one hand but a blessing on the other. And even Jews could still come to God. Three thousand Jews were saved on the Day of Pentecost (Acts 2:41).

c) A sign of authority

Who were the great messengers who preached this transition? Who were the men of God who spoke of the curse and the judgment? Who were the men of God who spoke of the blessing to come to all nations? The apostles and the prophets. And it was to them that God gave the ability to speak these languages as an authenticating, validating sign that what they were saying was indeed the truth. To the Jewish mind, the idea that God would make such a transition would be so shocking, so shattering, so incomprehensible, so stupendous, that there would have to be some kind of reinforcement that what they were saying was true. Therefore God gave them the ability to speak these languages.

In 1 Corinthians 14:18 Paul says, "I thank my God, I speak with tongues more than ye all." The gift of tongues authenticated Paul's position as an apostle, as well as the other sign gifts that he had. He even says in 2 Corinthians 12:12 that he had "the signs of an apostle . . . signs, and wonders, and mighty deeds." The gift of tongues was a sign of authority to those who preached the message of transition.

A good way to remember this threefold purpose of the gift of tongues is to remember it as the ABCs of the purpose of tongues: authority, blessing, and cursing. The purpose of tongues was not private devotions, evangelism, or a proof of Spirit baptism. The purpose of tongues was unique. Once the transition was made the church was born, Jerusalem was destroyed, and the sign was no longer necessary.

When Is a Sign No Longer Necessary?

When I take a trip I rely on signs to tell me how close I am to my destination. For example, if I'm driving north from Los Angeles to Sacramento, the first sign I see may indicate that I have 300 miles to go. The next sign may say 200 miles, then 150 miles, then 30 miles. Once I arrive in Sacramento, however, the signs will stop, because the purpose for the signs, as they point ahead to something, cease once the destination is reached. Tongues were a sign. They pointed to something—a curse of God upon Israel. And once the curse came, the sign was no longer necessary.

3. The priority of prophecy (v. 22b)

"But prophesying serveth not for them that believe not, but for them who believe."

Prophesying isn't restricted to unbelievers during a limited period of history; it is for believing people through all years of the church age. Tongues were a sign, pointing to something else; but prophesying is something in and of itself. The *New American Standard Bible* has the phrase "prophecy is for a sign" in verse 22. They put it in italics, indicating that it's not in the original, but nevertheless it's an unfortunate translation. Prophecy is not a sign! Prophesying is that which edifies. It always has a function. Verse 3 says, "He that prophesieth speaketh unto men to edification, and exhortation, and comfort." Verse 4 says, "He that prophesieth edifieth the church." And verse 1 says, "Desire spiritual gifts, but rather that ye may prophesy." What does it mean to prophesy? It simply means "to proclaim the Word of God."

The Corinthian church was characterized by hysterical, selfish, self-centered, ego-building confusion. Paul in effect said, "Cut all that stuff out. Tongues have a specific purpose for a specific time only. But when you meet together, seek to prophesy and proclaim the truth." It's far more important to preach the Word.

There is no record in the entire Bible of anything ever said by anyone in tongues. Do you know why? Because it was a sign that was meant to pass away. It had no lasting value, even in a revelatory sense. But on the other hand, Peter called the entire Bible "a more sure word of prophecy" (2 Pet. 1:19). There's no comparison between something that's a sign and something that's a reality.

Tongues are a sign to unbelieving Jews, attached irretrievably to one point in redemptive history. They served well to show that Christianity was not to be distinctly Jewish, but worldwide. They served to corroborate and authenticate the speakers and the messengers who brought that message. And they served to show Israel that they had again rejected God in unbelief and apostasy. People sometimes ask, "Don't you believe that tongues could have a purpose today?" No. If tongues were around today, they would still have to have the same purpose that they always had. And what point would there be in signifying today that God is moving away from Israel to open the gospel to the nations? He did that two thousand years ago. We don't need more information on that. It's already done.

Having stated the purpose of tongues, watch how Paul related it to the assembling together of the Corinthians.

C. The Purpose Scrutinized (vv. 23-25)

1. The results of tongues in the assembly (v. 23)

"If, therefore, the whole church be come together into one place, and all speak with tongues, and there come in those that are unlearned, or unbelievers, will they not say that ye are mad?"

Why would someone entering the Corinthian assembly believe they were mad? There are two reasons. First, if the person was a Gentile, he wouldn't understand the sign of tongues. Second, if the person was a Jewish unbeliever, the true gift of tongues wouldn't mean anything to him because of the chaotic way in which it was exercised. In verse 27 Paul states that when the true gift is used properly, there would only be two or three people in the entire church who would speak in tongues, and each one would do it in order—not all at the same time.

When an unbeliever came into the Corinthian assembly, he said, "These people are mad!" Plato is his dialogue to Phaedrus associated the Greek word for madness (*manikē*) with that for prophecy (*mantikē*) in describing the ecstatic experiences that were involved in pagan worship. In other words, an unbelieving Gentile would enter the Corinthian church and say, "This is no different than the temple of Diana!" And an unbelieving Jew who entered the church would say the same thing. You may say, "But tongues were supposed to be a sign to the Jews." Yes, that's true. But if it was exercised in a chaotic fashion, it wouldn't mean anything to them—even if it were the true gift used in the wrong way.

The gift of tongues was a specific gift, to be used at a specific time, in a specific way, with a specific person in mind, and with a specific intent. Apart from that, its significance is nonexistent. "On the other hand," Paul said, "instead of speaking in tongues in your assembly, prophesy."

2. The results of prophecy in the assembly (vv. 24-25)

"But if all prophesy [speak the Word of God], and there come in one that believeth not, or one unlearned, he is convicted of all, he is judged of all. And thus are the secrets of his heart made manifest; and so falling down on his face he will worship God, and report that God is in you of a truth."

Tongues are useless to edify either the church or an individual, and they're useless to evangelize. They were simply a pre-evangelism sign to a nation that it had been cursed. Paul said, "Rather than speaking in tongues, make sure that you are proclaiming God's Word. Then, when an unbeliever comes into your midst, some amazing things are going to happen."

a) Conviction—"He is convicted of all" means that he will experience guilt.

b) Judgment—"He is judged of all" means that the verdict will be rendered that he experiences guilt because he is guilty.

c) Exposure—"The secrets of his heart [will be] made manifest" means his sin will become apparent. It will be unmasked.

Then in humiliation, with a sense of self-condemnation, the response will be that of:

d) Worship—"Falling down on his face he will worship God, and report that God is in you." In other words, he will say, "I have found the true God here in your midst."

Paul's point is this: you're going to get results if you prophesy. Don't you want that to be the case in your fellowship? Don't you want the people who come into your fellowship to see God? You don't want confusion. You want to be obedient to God's pattern. This is a thrilling promise to a church that exalts the proclamation of God's Word. The impact will be tremendous. But a service of speaking in tongues will produce sterility in the congregation and confusion among the visitors.

The gift of tongues was limited and regulated for a time that has long since passed. And what we're seeing today, I'm afraid, is the Corinthian perversion all over again. I'm not questioning the motives of those who claim to have the gift of tongues. I'm saying that they have the same approach to an individual, private prayer language that was characteristic of the pagan mystery religions. I want to exalt the Word of God and lift it up. It is the "more sure word of prophecy" and contains the answers to everything we need. I hope you're devoted to the truth.

Someone I had been patiently discipling for three years called me and said, "I just had the greatest spiritual breakthrough I've ever had. Something happened in my life that has dramatically transformed me. I finally understand what you've been saying to me for three years. I want the Word of God so much that it's consuming me." Then he said, "I want you to know that if someone told me I would have to choose between my Bible and food and water, I would tell them to take the food and water and leave my Bible. That's my sustenance! I have to have it to live."

God help all of us to be people of the Book—not seeking experiences but seeking the truth; fruitful in our understanding; and ministering to each other that which edifies and builds up.

Focusing on the Facts

1. The Corinthian Christians believed the gift of tongues was for what (see p. 122)?
2. Why is it important to determine the biblical purpose for the gift of tongues (see pp. 122-23)?
3. According to most Pentecostals and charismatics, what is the major purpose for the gift of tongues? How does this view compare with the view of the Corinthian church (see pp. 123-24)?
4. Based on Paul's argument in 1 Corinthians 14, why can't tongues be defined as a self-edifying, devotional prayer language (see pp. 124-25)?
5. Discuss the possibility of evangelism as the purpose of tongues. Is this what occurred on the Day of Pentecost? Explain (see pp. 125-26).
6. Some people suggest that speaking in tongues is proof of being baptized by the Holy Spirit. What are the problems with this view (see pp. 126-27)?
7. What did Paul mean when he told the Corinthians to stop being children in their understanding? Why were they in this state (see pp. 127-28)?
8. In what ways were the Corinthians evil toward one another (see p. 128)?
9. According to 1 Corinthians 14:22, what is the purpose of tongues? Does this verse leave any room for the notion that the gift of tongues can be used as a private prayer language? Explain (see p. 129).
10. Basically, the purpose of tongues as a sign is threefold: a sign of _____, a sign of _____, and a sign of _____ (see p. 129).
11. What Old Testament passage does Paul quote in 1 Corinthians 14:21? Why (see pp. 129-30)?
12. Was the concept of tongues as a sign of cursing (or judgment) an unfamiliar one to the Jews that were present on the Day of Pentecost? Explain (see pp. 129-32).

13. If the speaking in tongues that occurred on the Day of Pentecost was a sign to unbelieving Jews of impending judgment, what were the specifics of that judgment, and when did it take place (see pp. 132-33)?
14. On what date did the purpose for the gift of tongues cease? Why (see pp. 132-34)?
15. How can tongues be seen as a sign of blessing (see p. 134)?
16. God gave the apostles and the prophets the gift of tongues for what unique purpose (see pp. 134-35)?
17. How does Paul compare tongues and prophecy in 1 Corinthians 14:22? Based on this comparison, which gift is superior? Why (see p. 136)?
18. Why isn't it possible that tongues could have a valid purpose today (see p. 137)?
19. Why would a visitor entering the Corinthian assembly believe they were mad (see pp. 137-38)?
20. What is the literal meaning of the Greek word translated "mad" in verse 23? What light does this shed on what was going on in the Corinthian assembly (see pp. 137-38)?
21. In 1 Corinthians 14:24-25 Paul describes the responses of an unbeliever who enters into a church where the proclamation of God's Word is emphasized. What steps lead to this response (see pp. 138-39)?

Pondering the Principles

1. Paul told the Corinthians to stop being children in their spiritual understanding and to grow up to be men (1 Cor. 14:20). On a scale of 1-10, how would you rate your spiritual understanding? What can a Christian do to increase his spiritual understanding? What steps are you taking—or will you commit to take—to become spiritually mature?

2. In the Old Testament, God constantly pleaded with His people to repent of their wicked ways. And when they didn't, He warned them of coming judgment—even then, giving them the opportunity to repent. But when they refused to repent, God always followed through with His promise of judgment. As Christians, God promises to discipline and chasten us when we disobey Him. Fortunately, He has given us the Holy Spirit to

convict us when we sin. And graciously He allows us the opportunity to continually confess our sin to Him. However, if we don't listen to His convictions, and we shut our ears to His warnings, we will suffer the consequences of that sin. In fact, sin that is not repented of can cause sickness and even death (see 1 Cor. 11:29-30; 1 John 5:16). Will you take a moment to examine your own life for any willful disobedience or defiance? Confess it, and then thank God for forgiving your sin and for cleansing you from all your unrighteousness (1 John 1:9).

7

The Truth About Tongues—Part 4

Outline

Introduction
A. The Emphasis of Edification
B. The Etymology of Edification
C. The Equal Responsibility of Edification
D. The Error of Self-Edification
E. The Elements of Edification
    1. The right attitude: selflessness
    2. The right tool: God's Word
    3. The right perspective: God's work
F. The Effect of Edification

Review
  I. The Position of the Gift of Tongues: It Is Secondary (vv. 1-19)
 II. The Purpose of the Gift of Tongues: It Is a Sign (vv. 20-25)

Lesson
III. The Procedure for the Gift of Tongues: It Is Systematic (vv. 26-40)
    A. The State of the Corinthians' Worship (v. 26)
        1. The overview
        2. The specifics
            a) "When ye come together"
            b) "Every one of you hath a psalm"
            c) "Hath a doctrine"
            d) "Hath a revelation"
            e) "Hath a tongue"
            f) "Hath an interpretation"

Introduction

A. The Emphasis of Edification

As we have noted in our earlier studies of 1 Corinthians 14, the key to this chapter is the word *edification*. Many times the actual word *edification* is used (or one of its various forms), and in some cases it is alluded to. For example, verse 3 speaks about edification; verse 4 speaks about edifying the church; verse 5 says, "That the church may receive edifying"; verse 12 says, "To the edifying of the church"; verse 19 says, "That by my voice I might teach others also"; and verse 26 sums up by saying, "Let all things be done unto edifying."

This, then, is the thought that is emphasized throughout this entire fourteenth chapter of 1 Corinthians. When the church comes together in corporate worship, the primary issue is that the people be edified.

B. The Etymology of Edification

Let's look for a moment at the word *edification*. The Greek verb *oikodomeō* and the Greek noun *oikodomē* both come from the combination of two words: *oikos*, which means "house," and *demō*, which means "to build." The word *edify/edification* literally means "to build a house/a house builder." To be edified, then, is to be built up. That's the term used in 1 Corinthians 14.

The word *oikodomē* is translated "builders" five times in the same statement in the New Testament: "The stone which the builders rejected, the same is become the head of the corner" (Matt. 21:42; cf. Mark 12:10; Luke 20:17; Acts 4:11; 1 Pet. 2:7). This is a metaphorical expression picturing Christ. The point, however, is that the word used there for builders, in all five cases, is a form of the word that is also translated edification. In a spiritual sense, edification is like building a house. The church is to have, as its intention and design, the building up of the saints into full completeness. To edify someone, then, means "to promote spiritual growth," "to develop the character of the believer to the place of real maturity."

C. The Equal Responsibility of Edification

The major element of the church is edification. We are to be edified together as a body. Even though we're to be edified when the church comes together to worship, it is also the responsibility of every believer to be actively involved in individually edifying one another. This is simply put by Paul in 1 Thessalonians 5:11, where he says, "Comfort yourselves together, and edify one another." It is not merely the task of the preacher or leader to edify the church; it is also the task of every believer.

Edification is the task of the leader as well. Ephesians 4:11-12 says, "He gave some, apostles; and some, prophets; and some, evangelists; and some, pastors and teachers; for the perfecting of the saints for the work of the ministry for the edifying of the body of Christ." The leadership and the people are involved together in building one another up to spiritual maturity. This is our calling, our God-given responsibility, our divine mandate—that which God seeks as the expression of His will in the church.

This presupposes that we are never to act selfishly. We are not to be concerned about our own successes, about our own glorification, or even about our own edification. Instead, we are to be lost in the edifying of one another. Romans 15:2 says, "Let every one of us please his neighbor for his good to edification." Then as an example verse 3 continues, "For even Christ pleased not himself." Christ came "not to be ministered unto but to minister, and to give his life a ransom for many" (Mark 10:45). Christ did not seek that which would be the most beneficial to Him, but that which would be most beneficial to others. And that is exactly what we are enjoined to do. We have a responsibility before God to edify each other.

D. The Error of Self-Edification

In 1 Corinthians 14:2 Paul points out an error rather than emphasizing a truth when he says to the Corinthians, "He that speaketh in an unknown tongue speaketh not unto men." That's what they should have been doing—speaking to men and edifying each other. In verse 4 he says, "He that speaketh in an unknown tongue edifieth himself." That was all wrong! The Bible never calls on us to edify ourselves. We're to edify each other.

E. The Elements of Edification

We are together for the purpose of building each other up. That involves several elements:

1. The right attitude: selflessness

To edify one another we must have a right attitude. Paul speaks of it in Romans 14:19 when he says, "Let us, therefore, follow after the things which make for peace,

146

and things with which one may edify another." In other words he says, "Pursue that which will build up someone else." Don't exercise your own liberty. Don't say, "I have every right to do thus and so because I'm under grace," or, "I don't care what anyone thinks; I'll do what I want," or, "I'll seek my own self-glorification," or, "I'll preach this sermon so they'll think I'm really something. Then I can make a name for myself," or, "I'll do what I do for my own good." Those attitudes violate the right attitude, which is seeking to edify one another.

2. The right tool: God's Word

If you're going to edify one another, there's only one tool that's effective—the Word of God. Second Timothy 3:16-17 says the Word of God is able to build us up and make us perfect, or complete. We are responsible, then, to have an attitude that seeks the other's good and to use the Word of God to teach each other.

3. The right perspective: God's work

I believe we must have patience with one another and let God do His work in His own time.

F. The Effect of Edification

We are to be committed to edifying one another as we meet together. You may ask, "But where does evangelism fit into the picture? How can we reach out to others if all we're doing is edifying the saints?" The answer to that is in Acts 9:31, which says, "Then had the churches rest throughout all Judaea and Galilee and Samaria, and were edified [they were doing what they should have been doing: being edified and built up to maturity]; and walking in the fear of the Lord, and in the comfort of the Holy Spirit, were multiplied." Growth is a result of edification. As the church is built up, it will reach out. Evangelism will be a by-product of edification.

We're to meet together to be edified. We're to meet together to be taught the Word of God and exposed to God's truth in a way that will cause us to grow to maturity. Edification is the priority of the church.

Review

In the Corinthian church, the whole procedure of edification had come to a halt. Edification was nonexistent because of the confusion and the disorder with which they were functioning. In 1 Corinthians 14 Paul tries to call a halt to the perversion, the counterfeit, and the confusion, and bring the Corinthians back to a system of order that would grant them edification.

In 14:1-25 Paul lays out some of the principles relative to how tongues and prophesying should function, as well as what they are in terms of their purpose and position. He also gives us some clear theological definitions. Beginning in verse 26, he builds on those theological definitions with practical exhortations. In other words he says, "Since this is true of these gifts, this is the way you should act."

I. THE POSITION OF THE GIFT OF TONGUES: IT IS SECONDARY (vv. 1-19; see pp. 83-94, 102-18)

II. THE PURPOSE OF THE GIFT OF TONGUES: IT IS A SIGN (vv. 20-25; see pp. 123-40)

Lesson

III. THE PROCEDURE FOR THE GIFT OF TONGUES: IT IS SYSTEMATIC (vv. 26-40)

A. The State of the Corinthians' Worship (v. 26)

"How is it then, brethren? When ye come together, everyone of you hath a psalm, hath a doctrine, hath a tongue, hath a revelation, hath an interpretation. Let all things be done unto edifying."

1. The overview

   Paul is basically saying, "How is it, knowing what you know about the foolishness of confusion, that all of you are doing these things all at the same time and in the same place?" Paul was not telling the Corinthians to do what is listed in verse 26; he was simply detailing for them what they were already doing. They all were vying for preeminence. And those who were using counterfeit or nonexistent gifts were thrown into this mishmash. No one could have been edified in their services if he had tried. In fact, unbelievers concluded that the Corinthian Christians were out of their minds!

2. The specifics

   a) "When ye come together"

   This phrase indicates a church in its assemblage when it comes together for its corporate time of worship and fellowship. Verse 23 also indicates that this is when the whole church gathers together. In other words, if you attended church in Corinth on any given Sunday, you'd experience the following:

   b) "Every one of you hath a psalm"

   When we see the word *psalm* we usually think of a psalm from the Old Testament book of Psalms. And it's possible that some of the people in the Corinthian church may have wanted to read one of those psalms out loud to the congregation. However, the Greek word used here literally means "a song sung to the accompaniment of an instrument." More likely, what was going on in the Corinthian church was several people singing a solo at the same time.

   Can you imagine the chaos of a situation like that? Anyone who wanted to sing a solo started to sing to the accompaniment of someone plucking along on a stringed instrument or someone blowing a flute. Imagine the dissonance resulting from all that!

Psalms were a common part of Christian worship. Colossians 3:16 mentions "psalms and hymns and spiritual songs." In fact, the ministry of music was not something added to the church at a later date. It existed from the first time the church began to meet in the New Testament. Singing has always been a wonderful part of Christian worship. But in Corinth it became a point of pride; everyone was trying to out-sing everyone else.

c) "Hath a doctrine"

"Hath a doctrine" simply means "a teaching" or "a lesson." Everyone who wanted to exercise the gift of teaching—every would-be teacher—stood up in his own corner and began giving his lesson. Over the din of one group singing solos was another group giving lessons—teaching whatever it was they believed the church needed to hear.

d) "Hath a revelation"

There were people standing up in the congregation and saying, "Thus saith the Lord," and then proclaiming some great supposed revelation they were having. Of course, they had to do it over the noise of the people who were trying to teach their lessons and sing their solos.

e) "Hath a tongue"

There were people who were standing up and speaking with the gift of languages—legitimately, but out of order and in the wrong place. It was the true gift in a wrong expression. And there were others who didn't have the true gift of tongues who were mumbling gibberish.

I mentioned that when the word *tongue* appears earlier in this chapter in the singular form, it has reference to the false gift, because gibberish can't be plural. However, in verses 26 and 27 the singular word *tongue* could have reference to the true gift, because it's merely singling out that one of them has a tongue. In other words, it could be translated, "One of you has a language," referring to the true gift, just as easily as it could be translated, "One of you has gibberish—a counterfeit." The use of the singular word *tongue* is demanded here because the subject of the verse is singular. The same thing is true in verse 27, as we shall see. That doesn't violate my premise that where the word *tongues* appears in the plural it is referring to the true gift and the singular word *tongue* refers to the false, counterfeit gift. When the singular word is demanded by a singular subject, it could be referring to either the true or the false gift.

f) "Hath an interpretation"

These people were attempting to interpret whatever was going on—and probably fighting and arguing about which interpretation was right.

All of this was the order of worship in the Corinthian church. Now you can understand why unbelievers who came in and saw all this going on said, "These people are out of their minds! What kind of craziness is this?" At the end of verse 26, Paul calls a halt to the chaos and says, "Let all things be done unto edifying." This is a key statement. He's saying, "The way to resolve all this confusion is to edify—to build one another up" in an orderly fashion. Then in verses 27-35 he shows them how to do that.

B. The Structure for the Corinthians' Edification (vv. 27-35)

1. The procedure for tongues (vv. 27-28)

Verse 27 begins, "If any man speak in an unknown tongue." Notice that the subject is singular, as it was in verse 26. Unfortunately, the King James translators added the word *unknown*. I believe this is the one time they added it when they shouldn't have, because I believe he's talking here about the true gift. I believe Paul is referring to the true gift here because it has already been made clear that he would never regulate gibberish. Gibberish was to be totally eliminated—not regulated. Only the true gift could be regulated.

a) Principle 1 (v. 27*b*)

"Let it be by two, or at the most by three."

Every gift that has ever been given by God is subject to the control of the possessor. The Holy Spirit never does anything through someone who is out of control. The Spirit of God ministers the gifts through people who are characterized by self-control, which is one of the fruits of the Spirit (Gal. 5:23). Spiritual gifts are not like the pagan ecstasies, which were totally out of the control of the individual. That's why we find principles in Scripture on how to apply the gifts.

How were the people with the real gift of languages regulated? Someone in the congregation would tell a person with the gift when there was an unbelieving Jew in their midst that spoke a certain foreign language. Then the person with the gift would look around to make sure that someone with the gift of interpretation was also present. In the right place at the right time, the one with the gift of languages would speak that language—a language unknown to him but known to that Jewish unbeliever. The message, then, would reach that Jewish person, the interpreter would interpret it for the edification of the congregation, and it would be used in its proper manner.

The gift of tongues was always to be used under control. And the first limiting factor was that there were never to be more than two, or at the very most three, people using this gift. It was a gift reserved for those special times when both an unbelieving Jew and an interpreter were there. And it never was to occur more than three times on any given occasion. That was the limit.

That is not what is done today in the tongues movement. They do not have such limitations. They do not limit their tongues speaking on the basis of an unbelieving Jew being present, they do not limit it on the basis of a legitimate language being spoken, and they do not limit it to two or three at a time. There may be some isolated cases where these guidelines are followed, but in most cases they are not. What we have today is the Corinthian problem all over again—the problem that ignores these basic features.

b) Principle 2 (v. 27*c*)

"And that by course."

The Greek means "in turn," "in order," or "in sequence." The Corinthians were involved in simultaneously expressing their gifts, as I've pointed out. That is forbidden, but is precisely what goes on so frequently in tongues meetings today, where everyone is speaking in tongues all at the same time. Have you ever noticed on charismatic television programs that when the people begin to pray in tongues, they all do it at the same time? It's normal procedure in almost all charismatic churches for everyone to pray in tongues at the same time.

c) Principle 3 (v. 27*d*)

"And let one interpret."

Here is something most people miss. The Greek text emphasizes the word translated "one" (*heis*) in this verse by putting it in the emphatic form. The verse is saying, "Let one interpret—not two, five, seven, or fourteen—just one." Why? Because the problem in the Corinthian church was that everyone wanted to gain the preeminence by giving the interpretation. Consequently, there were often fights about whose interpretation was correct.

Paul in effect said, "I'll settle the problem you're having with tongues. Only two, or three at the most, are to speak in tongues—and always in sequence. Furthermore, only one person with the gift of interpretation is to interpret." That takes care of the problem. But what if there isn't an interpreter around to give the interpretation?

d) Principle 4 (v. 28)

"But if there be no interpreter, let him keep silence in the church; and let him speak to himself, and to God."

In other words, if you had the true gift of tongues and an unbelieving Jew came into the assembly but there wasn't anyone around with the gift of interpretation, you were to sit and meditate. "Why?" you may ask. "It could be a great evangelistic tool!" Yes, but if there wasn't anyone there who could translate, it wouldn't have any capacity to edify the church. And the purpose for the church's meeting together is edification. So when no one was there to translate, you would have to remain silent.

This verse also tells me that the Corinthians were supposed to know who in their congregation had the true gift of interpretation. If none of them were there, the only alternative for those with the gift of tongues was to remain silent. There are no legitimate instances of someone speaking in tongues when no one is able to understand what is being said. And if such a case were ever to present itself in the church, it was to be stopped immediately. If there was no interpreter present, the tongues speaker was to be quiet. He was to sit there, meditate, and talk to God in prayer. But he was not to say anything out loud.

These principles do a good job of regulating tongues. In fact, if the true gift of tongues hadn't ceased in the first century, these regulations might end 95 percent of what goes on in the tongues movement today.

2. The procedure for prophesying (vv. 29-33*a*)

One might believe that because the gift of prophesying was such a grandiose and exalted gift, it never fell into abuse. But it did. Therefore Paul had to set down some principles for regulating this gift. In verses 29-33*a*, he addresses the gift of prophesying, which was vital to the early church. Apparently people in the Corinthian church were jumping up and saying they had a word from the Lord that they wanted to proclaim. They wanted to give a good statement from God and preach a great truth. To harnass the potential chaos into some kind of order that could edify the people, Paul wrote four principles to regulate the procedure for prophesying in the church.

a) Principle 1 (v. 29*a*)

"Let the prophets speak two or three."

This is the same principle that regulated speaking in tongues. There were never to be more than three prophets speaking in one service. One was great, two were OK, but three was the maximum number.

(1) The prophets' description

You may ask, "Who are the prophets that are mentioned here in 1 Corinthians 14? Are these Old Testament prophets?" No, these are New Testament prophets. The word translated "prophet" comes from two Greek words, *pro* and *phēmi*, and literally means "someone who speaks before." The prophets, then, were men who spoke before the people. They were those who stood up to declare God's message.

(2) The prophets' declaration

The prophets spoke in two ways. They spoke direct revelation from God that had never been given, and they reiterated messages that had already been given by the apostles. Apparently the church

155

service was structured so that one, two, or at the most three prophets could be the ones who spoke God's message.

(3) The prophets' disappearance

The prophets were foundational. They're not mentioned later in the church. For example, when Paul wrote certain epistles to set the churches in order (1 and 2 Timothy and Titus), he never mentions prophets. He simply talks about elders, presbyters, bishops, deacons, and deaconesses. That's all he ever talks about because prophets passed away with the passing of the apostolic age. They were a unique group. Ephesians 2:20 says that they were given for the foundation of the church. They belonged to that time.

The prophets were to speak God's message. Sometimes they spoke messages that they had prepared, and sometimes they spoke direct revelation from God that they had received. Either way, they were to speak—but never more than two or three at one service. Why? Because anything more than that would be chaotic, and there would be a constant fight to see who would be able to stand up and speak.

b) Principle 2 (v. 29b)

"And let the others judge."

"Others" refers to the other prophets. They were to evaluate the truth of what he was saying. It might well be that these prophets had the gift of discernment (see 1 Cor. 12:10). In other words, they were given the ability to discern whether something was of God or not. They were there to evaluate the truth of the message. People were not to speak without someone's evaluating it.

This principle highlights a problem in charismatic churches today. When someone stands up in a church and says, "I have the gift of prophecy and a revelation from God," and then proceeds to give his revelation, what criteria does the church have to know whether or not what he says is of God? The criteria in that day were men of God who were divinely granted the ability to discern truth from error. It had to be that way, because they didn't have the written Word that we now have.

We don't need any more revelations today. The complete revelation is here. And when people today have what they claim are new revelations, they're in a dangerous position. It's far better to stop with the last part of the book of Revelation and not risk the curse of adding to Scripture described therein (22:18).

Who Were the Leaders of the Corinthian Church?

Apparently the Corinthian church didn't have any of the people that are designated as leaders in the pastoral epistles—elders, bishops, presbyters, or pastor-teachers. None are ever indicated. They did have prophets, however. But they were only for that foundational time of the church.

c) Principle 3 (v. 30)

> "If anything be revealed to another [prophet] that sitteth by, let the first [prophet] hold his peace."

This is most interesting. Let's say a prophet was giving a message that he had prepared, when all of a sudden God gave a new revelation to one of the other prophets. The prophet with the new revelation was to immediately pull the tunic of the prophet speaking, and say, "God just gave me a new revelation." At that point, the prophet that was speaking had to sit down. Why? Because a new revelation always took precedence over reiterating something that had

157

already been given. God had special words for His church that had never been given.

This reinforces a point I've been trying to make all along. Some say that the prophets spoke new revelation only. But I believe they spoke either revelation or reiteration. This verse is one of the strongest proofs of that because it describes a prophet who is reiterating and who has to sit down if another prophet gets a new revelation. It's reasonable, then, to see that some prophets received new revelation on occasion, whereas others were simply reiterating a message that was no less from God but not a fresh, new revelation for the moment.

At this point one of the Corinthian prophets was probably saying, "Paul, I don't know if I can do that. When I get under the power of the Holy Spirit, the words just come out. I can't control it." Therefore Paul gives another principle in verses 31-32.

d) Principle 4 (vv. 31-32)

"For ye may all prophesy one by one, that all may learn and all may be comforted. And the spirits of the prophets are subject to the prophets."

Paul's point is this: If you're a true prophet, you will be able to control the gift. A true gift never functions in pagan ecstasy. True gifts always function under the control of the individual.

Paul gave the prophets some simple principles to follow. Why? The purpose was always the same: "That all may learn, and all may be comforted." The edification of the church is the issue. No one is edified if there is nothing but disorder and chaos. Paul in essence said, "Don't give me the excuse that you're out of control." Incidentally, the Greek word translated "spirits" is the same word translated "spiritual gifts" in verse 12 of this chapter. In other words, he's saying, "Your gift of prophecy is under the control of the other prophets, so you can't operate in an uncontrolled manner."

At the beginning of verse 33 Paul sums up his discussion on the procedure for prophesying with a beautiful truth. He says, "God is not the author of confusion but of peace." This is the key to the whole chapter. The worship service of the church should manifest the character of God. "When you come together," Paul said, "all that is part of your service should be manifesting the God whom we serve. Our God is not a God of confusion. He is a God of peace. When someone comes into your church and sees confusion and fighting for preeminence, he will conclude that you have a confused, contentious God."

I'm afraid there are people who see what goes on in many charismatic circles today and conclude that the God they worship is in the same state of chaos. However, God is a God of order and dignity. He is a God who functions systematically for results, not chaotically for feelings. And that characteristic of God is to be manifested properly in the worship of His church.

3. The procedure for women (vv. 33b-35)

    "As in all churches of the saints. Let your women keep silence in the churches; for it is not permitted unto them to speak, but they are commanded to be under obedience, as also saith the law. And if they will learn anything, let them ask their husbands at home; for it is a shame for women to speak in the church."

    I believe the end of verse 33 should be attached to verse 34. My main reason is that it doesn't make sense to connect the great, sweeping, theological truth that "God is not the author of confusion but of peace" with the words "as in all churches of the saints." God is not a God of confusion but of peace. Period. Not just in the churches of the saints.

159

Why does Paul all of a sudden bring up the subject of women in the church? It appears that the women in the Corinthian assembly were leading the parade to seek the showy gifts as well as usurping the place of leadership in the congregation. The women were not being silent and submissive in the church; they were trying to take over the service.

a) The woman's silence

  (1) Is it cultural?

    I hear people say, "You know that teaching in 1 Corinthians 14 about women keeping silent in the church? That was just a Corinthian problem —strictly a cultural thing. Paul was just trying to accommodate to the Corinthian culture." If you believe that, look again at verses 33*b*-34*a*. Paul said, "As in all churches of the saints. Let your women keep silence in the churches." It isn't a Corinthian cultural issue; it's to be the standard in all the churches. In the Corinthian church women were speaking in tongues, interpreting, singing their songs, prophesying, and usurping male authority. Paul singled them out and reminded them that women are to take the place of submission and silence in the public service of the church.

    God has gifted women in marvelous ways. Many of them have the gifts of teaching and proclaiming God's Word. But they are not to exercise those particular gifts in the mixed assembly of the church when it comes together. That belongs to men, as we soon shall see.

    Again this is not a cultural issue. Notice at the end of verse 34 why women are not permitted to speak in the church.

  (2) Is it commanded?

    Verse 34 says, "It is not permitted unto them to speak, but they are commanded to be under obedience, as also saith the law." What law? The law of God—the Pentateuch. Genesis 3:16 says that the man will rule over the woman. Even before the Fall we see the man in authority and the woman in submission in a non-threatening way (Gen. 2:18).

In 1 Timothy 2:11-12 Paul says, "Let the woman learn in silence with all subjection. But I permit not a woman to teach, nor to usurp authority over the man, but to be in silence." Why? Not because of the culture of Ephesus or because of a problem in Timothy's town. Verses 13-14 give us the reason: "For Adam was first formed, then Eve. And Adam was not deceived, but the woman, being deceived, was in the transgression." In other words, this is a divine design from the beginning. You can't get rid of it on the basis of culture. It is in the law of God.

b) The woman's shame

In verse 35 Paul says, "It is a shame for women to speak in the church." The Greek word translated "shame" (*aischros*) literally means "ugly" or "deformed." In other words, for a woman to speak in the church is a deformity of God's intention—a perversion of beauty into ugliness.

Many women are excellent teachers, and they should be busy teaching other women—in the right place at the right time. But the right place and the right time is not the assembly of the church. I thank God for gifted women who teach other women, and for older women who teach younger women to be godly, as Paul told Titus to instruct them to do (Titus 2:3-5). We must obey God's standards. Husbands are to love and lead, and wives are to submit and respond. In fact, the husband-wife relationship is analogous to the relationship between Christ and the church (Eph. 5:22-32). The principles of authority and submission are a reflection of God's order and nature. When that doesn't exist in His church, the revealing of His order and His nature is violated. For example, God cannot be on display in a church where a woman is preaching. Why? Simply because His nature, His plan, and His purpose are violated—even though the woman may say good things.

c) The woman's source

According to verse 35, if a woman has questions she is to go home and ask her husband. That puts the responsibility on the husbands to find out answers. But that's the way God has designed it. Husbands, don't be content to give a standard answer of, "I don't know." Get some answers, and be the spiritual leader in your home.

d) The woman's speaking out

Notice the phrase "if they will learn anything" in verse 35. I believe this is saying that some of the women were asking questions in the service under false pretenses. They were blurting out their questions to confront the prophet who was speaking. They were interrupting the prophet (and the service) on the pretense of having a legitimate question when, in actuality, they just wanted to be heard. According to verses 29-30, apparently the only ones who had the right to ask questions in the service were the prophets. These women were usurping the place of the prophets, who had the responsibility of discerning what was being said.

I don't believe Paul was saying that women are never to ask spiritual questions of anyone other than their husbands. There's nothing wrong when questions are asked in the sharing together of Bible study and fellowship. In fact, when we have a question-and-answer session in our church, I believe it's proper for anyone to ask a question—because that's the order of the time. But during the duly constituted worship service of the church, when there is structure and order for the edification of the whole body, we are to follow these patterns. A public worship service is never to be interrupted and usurped by a woman asking a question. Can you imagine those prophets in the Corinthian church trying to get through their messages with everyone trying to argue with them?

C. The Sarcasm to Elicit the Corinthians' Acceptance (v. 36)

Paul was strong about these procedures for the regulation of women, tongues, and prophecy in the church—so strong that he responds in verse 36 to their anticipated resistance to what he had to say. He said, "What? Came the word of God out from you? Or came it unto you only?" In other words, "Do you want to argue about this? Did you write the Word of God? Or did it just come to you? Are you some kind of a law unto yourselves?" I believe Paul was being slightly sarcastic with them to get them to respond to and accept his words, saying, "Did you write the Bible? Either you are the ones who wrote it, or you are required to submit to it. Those are the only options. Now if you're not going to obey it, maybe you believe you wrote it. Or maybe you believe it doesn't apply to you—just everyone else. Since the same Scripture applies to you that applies to everyone, and since it's all authored by God, you have only one response: to obey." Paul called a halt to all their selfish activity and said, "Do only that which edifies."

D. The Summary of Paul's Exhortation (vv. 37-40)

1. Acknowledge it as a commandment of God (v. 37)

"If any man think himself to be a prophet, or spiritual [which I believe refers to the gift of tongues because it's the sum of what Paul is saying], let him acknowledge that the things that I write unto you are the commandments of the Lord."

This is a great closing statement. It clinches the whole argument. He in effect said, "Those who have legitimate gifts will acknowledge that I speak the Word of God. And if they acknowledge that I speak the Word of God, they will bring their gifts under submission to the

163

principles I've just spoken. If they don't, they don't have the true gift. What they're doing is not a legitimate manifestation of the Holy Spirit." Paul was trying to get the Corinthians to see that if the gifts of tongues and prophecy weren't used according to the regulations he had laid down in verses 27-33, those in violation were not legitimate.

One of the greatest claims Paul ever made to being inspired by God is the statement that he makes in verse 37: "The things that I write unto you are the commandments of the Lord." I'll never forget meeting a man who believed only the red letters in his Bible. I've never liked red-letter Bibles since. He believed that the words in red, which indicate the statements of Jesus in the gospels, were the only important words. I told him that the words of Paul as just as important as the words of Jesus. Then I showed him this passage: "The things that I write unto you are the commandments of the Lord."

Don't try to pass off Paul's teaching as cultural or only opinion. I hear people say, "Women don't have to be silent in the church. Women can preach if they want to. Paul's words in 1 Corinthians 14 are only cultural." I also hear them say, "We don't have to follow all these different regulations about tongues and prophesying today, because those regulations were only for Corinth." No. These are God's commandments for everyone.

2. Reject those who ignore it (v. 38)

In verse 38 Paul recognizes that there are going to be some people who are going to ignore his commandments: "But if any man be ignorant, let him be ignorant." The meaning of the verse is this: "If anyone ignores these things, you ignore him." In other words, if a person didn't recognize that Paul's regulations were the Word of God, then that person couldn't be recognized as having the true gift. Therefore, that person was to be rejected because he was a phony.

3. Desire prophecy in the church (v. 39)

In verse 39 Paul summarizes by saying, "Wherefore, brethren, covet to prophesy, and forbid not to speak with tongues." In other words, "On the basis of all that I've said, zealously desire to prophesy." Why? Because "he that prophesieth speaketh unto men to edification and exhortation, and comfort" (v. 3). Then Paul said, "Forbid not to speak with tongues." For that time and that age there was a true gift of languages. And even though the gift of prophecy was to be emphasized in the church, Paul was not forbidding the use of a true gift in its true expression at its true time. Now this cannot be applied to today, because the true gift of tongues has ceased. But for that time Paul said, "I recognize the true gift of tongues, and I'm not forbidding you to use it. It has its place. But when you come together in the church, seek to prophesy."

4. Let the church service manifest God's character (v. 40)

Summing it up, Paul said, "Let all things be done decently and in order." The word *decently* refers to harmony and beauty, and the word *order* refers to things being done in sequence. Since God is a God of harmony, beauty, and order, Paul said, "Let your assembling together manifest those characteristics of God." And as the church manifests God and is edified, it will also be multiplied. That's God promise.

Focusing on the Facts

1. What key word shows the emphasis of 1 Corinthians 14? What is the literal meaning of this word (see pp. 144-45)?
2. The intention and design of the church is to _____ _____ the saints (see p. 145).

3. Whose responsibility is it to make sure the church is being edified? Support your answer biblically (see pp. 145-46).
4. What three elements are involved in being able to edify one another properly (see pp. 146-47)?
5. Should edification or evangelism be the priority in the church? Explain (see p. 147).
6. Why was edification nonexistent in the Corinthian church (see p. 148)?
7. If you had visited a church service in Corinth during the time of Paul, what would you have experienced, according to 1 Corinthians 14:26? Describe each of the specifics listed (see pp. 148-51).
8. Tongues are mentioned in verse 26. Do we know whether this is referring to the true gift or the counterfeit gift? Explain (see pp. 150-51).
9. Why must the tongues of verse 27 be referring to the legitimate gift of tongues (see pp. 151-52)?
10. What are the four principles given by Paul in 1 Corinthians 14:27-28 to regulate the use of the gift of tongues? Are they followed by charismatic fellowships today? Explain (see pp. 152-54).
11. What does it mean that tongues were to be spoken "by course" (see p. 153)?
12. What is the significance of the word *one* in 1 Corinthians 14:27 (see p. 153)?
13. What was the tongues speaker to do if his gift could have been used to speak to an unbelieving Jew who had entered the church, but an interpreter wasn't present (see p. 154)?
14. Why couldn't a person with the true gift of tongues exercise his gift without someone's being present who had the gift of interpretation? How was he to know whether an interpreter was present (see p. 154)?
15. If the gift of tongues hadn't ceased in the first century, how much of the tongues speaking that goes on today might be eliminated solely on the basis of the four principles given by Paul in 1 Corinthians 14:27-28 (see p. 154)?
16. Why did the gift of prophesying have to be regulated in the Corinthian church? What were the four principles regulating this gift (see pp. 155-59; 1 Cor. 14:29-33a)?
17. What are the two types of messages that the New Testament prophets declared (see pp. 155-56)?
18. Why weren't the prophets mentioned by Paul when he wrote about the leadership of the church in the pastoral epistles (see p. 156)?

166

19. In the early church when the prophets spoke, who evaluated whether or not what they said was true? What was their criteria (see pp. 156-57)?

20. Why doesn't the church need any more direct revelation from God? What is the danger of someone's standing up and saying that he has a direct message from God (see p. 157)?

21. Who were the leaders of the Corinthian church (see p. 157)?

22. If a prophet was speaking a message that he had prepared, and one of the other prophets interrupted him by saying he had just received a new revelation from God, what was the first prophet to do? Why (see pp. 157-58)?

23. What is the point that Paul is making in 1 Corinthians 14:32 (see p. 158)?

24. Why did Paul consider it imperative for the Corinthians to have principles regulating their gifts, according to 14:33a (see p. 159)?

25. Why should 14:33b actually be attached to 14:34 instead of 14:33a (see pp. 159-60)?

26. Why did Paul bring up the subject of women in the church in the midst of a discussion on the regulation of prophecy and tongues (see p. 160)?

27. Was the silence that women were to maintain in the church strictly a cultural regulation? Was it merely to be applied to the Corinthian church? Explain (see pp. 160-61).

28. Are women to keep silent in the church today? Why or why not (see p. 161)?

29. Why is it shameful for a women to speak in the church? Does this mean a woman cannot have the gift of teaching? Explain (see pp. 161-62).

30. According to verse 35, if a woman has questions in church, she is to seek the answers from whom? This places the responsibility on whom (see p. 162)?

31. Why were the women asking questions in the Corinthian assembly (see p. 162)?

32. Explain Paul's sarcasm in verse 36 (see p. 163).

33. How do we know that the regulations that Paul put on tongues, prophecy, and women in the church are not merely his opinions (see pp. 163-64)?

34. If someone were to ignore Paul's regulations, what conclusions could be made regarding the authenticity of his gift? This person was to be dealt with in what manner (see pp. 164-65)?

35. What gift was to receive the primary emphasis in the Corinthian church? Why? Did this mean that the gift of tongues was not to be exercised in their assembly? Why (see p. 165)?

36. Why can't the last part of verse 39 apply to us today (see p. 165)?

37. What does it mean for all things to be done "decently and in order"? Why is this essential (see p. 165)?

Pondering the Principles

1. It is the task of every believer to be involved in edifying one another (Rom. 14:19; 15:2; 1 Thess. 5:11). What does it mean to edify someone? What are some ways we can accomplish this? What are you presently doing to edify others in the Body of Christ?

2. The worship service of the church is to manifest the character of God. When a stranger comes into your church, what characteristics of God does he see? What does he see that falsely represents God? What can you personally do to see that God is accurately manifested in your worship service?

3. What did Paul mean when he said that women were to keep silent in the church? Did this simply refer to the Corinthian women in the Corinthian church? Explain. How does this apply to the trend today of women in the pulpit? Should a woman who is mature spiritually and gifted in teaching take over preaching in a church where there isn't a man available to do the job? How should women who are gifted in teaching exercise their gifts?

4. Based on all you have learned in this series on 1 Corinthians 13:8–14:40, what would you say to a Christian who came to you to find some scriptural answers to the issue of speaking in tongues? To organize your thinking on this whole issue, go back through the outline points in each chapter; then write down why, according to the Bible, tongues are not for today.

Scripture Index

Topical Index

Anderson, Sir Robert, on experience of tongues, 80-81
Augustine, on cessation of tongues, 26

Bible. *See* Scripture

Cevenols, tongues and, 27-28
Charismatic movement
attitude to have regarding, 13, 30, 32, 36, 52-53, 56, 98
controversy of, 53
extrabiblical revelation. *See* Scripture, completion of
importance of examining, 53
knowledge and. *See* Knowledge, gift of
miracles and. *See* Miracles
origin of, 29
prophecy and. *See* Prophecy, gift of
tongues and. *See* Tongues
Christenson, Larry, on purpose of tongues, 90, 124
Chrysostom, on cessation of tongues, 26
Church
Corinthian. *See* Corinthian church
main point of, 13. *See also* Love
ministry of. *See* Spiritual gifts
music in, 113, 149-50
mystery of, 134
orderliness of, 14, 159, 165, 168
women's role in. *See* Women

Clement of Rome, on cessation of tongues, 25
Controversial issues, dealing with, 53
Corinthian church
abuse of spiritual gifts, 14-15, 88
anti-intellectualism of, 128
chaos of, 149-65
corruption of, 9-10, 101, 119-20
leadership of, 14, 157
pagan practices of, 78-83, 87-88, 99-100, 122
pride of, 88, 101
selfishness of, 99-101, 109, 117, 122, 127-29, 148
unloving nature of, 10-11
worldliness of, 10, 32, 101

Death, fate of believers after, 72-73
Dillow, Joseph, on pagan practices of speaking in tongues, 46

Edification
definition of, 145
evangelism and, 147-48
importance of, 86-92, 102, 144-48
process of, 145-47
responsibility of, 145-46
See also Spiritual gifts
Eternal state, characteristics of, 71-72
Evangelism
edification and, 147-48
tongues and, 125-26

Moody Press, a ministry of the Moody Bible Institute, is designed for education, evangelization, and edification. If we may assist you in knowing more about Christ and the Christian life, please write us without obligation: Moody Press, c/o MLM, Chicago, Illinois 60610.